My First Golden Dictionary

By Ellen Wales Walpole

Illustrated by Gertrude Elliott

A special note to parents and teachers
appears on page 94.

HAMLYN
LONDON · NEW YORK · SYDNEY · TORONTO

FIRST PUBLISHED 1966 TWELFTH IMPRESSION 1979
BY THE HAMLYN PUBLISHING GROUP LIMITED
ASTRONAUT HOUSE, FELTHAM, MIDDLESEX, ENGLAND
BY ARRANGEMENT WITH WESTERN PUBLISHING COMPANY, INC. ALL RIGHTS RESERVED.
ISBN 0 601 07326 6
Printed by Litografía A. Romero, S. A. - Canary Islands (Spain).
D. L.: TF. 743 - 1979

eating

reading

walking

pushing

jumping

skipping

sleeping

climbing

hopping

running

singing

washing

writing

skating

kicking

pulling

digging

building

dancing

drinking

painting

sewing

swimming

dressing

sliding

These are **acts**.

4

A a

The first letter in the alphabet

a

Here are **a** pear and **an** apple.

an

a pear

an apple

able

John is **able** to touch his toes.
Ann is not **able** to touch her toes.

about

1. They ran **about** the beach.
   They ran all over the beach.
2. The story is **about** a duck.
   The story is of a duck.
3. It is **about** time to go to bed.
   It is almost time to go to bed.

above

The aircraft is **above** the clouds.

across

1. The pen is **across** the pencil.
2. The dog goes **across** the street.

act

1. **Acts** are things we do.
2. The players **act** on the stage.

acts   acted   acting

add

Add two apples and three apples.
You will have five apples.

$$2 + 3 = 5$$

adds   added   adding

afraid

The cat is **afraid** to jump.

after

1. The dog ran **after** the cat.
2. **After** school we run and play.

again

If at first you don't succeed,
try, try **again**.

against

1. Bob is leaning **against** the tree.
2. The goats are fighting
   against each other.

age

Grandfather's **age** is fifty-three years.
Polly's **age** is seven years.
Baby's **age** is four months.

ago

Ago means in the past.
Many years **ago** grandmother was

a little girl.

agree

I think cats are nice.

You think cats are bad.

We do not **agree** about cats.

agrees   agreed   agreeing

air

There is a covering of **air**
around our earth.

We breathe **air**.

Birds fly in the **air**.

aircraft

An **aircraft** is a flying machine.

It can fly over land and water.

all

Henry drank **all** his milk.

Baby did not drink **all** her milk.

almost

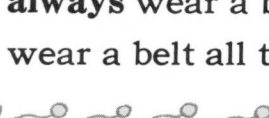

1. They ate **almost** all of the pie.
2. John **almost** caught a fish.

alone

The little bear is **alone** on the shelf.

I went outdoors **alone**.

No one was with me.

alphabet

There are 26 letters in our **alphabet**.

They are ABCDEFGHIJKLMNOPQRSTUVWXYZ.

already

Have you read the book **already?**

Have you read the book so soon?

also

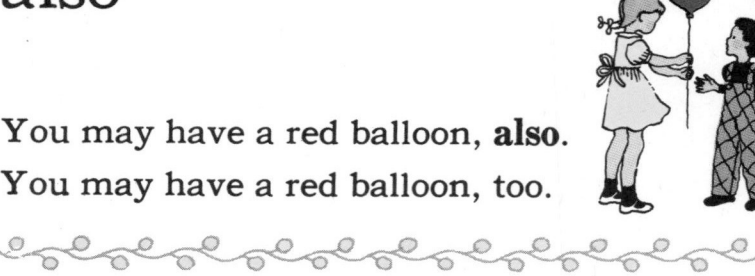

You may have a red balloon, **also**.

You may have a red balloon, too.

always

They **always** take their lunch to school.

They take their lunch to school
every day.

I **always** wear a belt.

I wear a belt all the time.

among

1. We divided the ice cream
   among the children.
2. The pigs are running **among** the chickens.

and

Jane **and** Bill have a cat **and** a dog.

angry

Do not poke the stick at the lion.

He will get **angry**.

animals

Animals are living things that move about.
They need food to keep alive.

kitten

cat

rat

dog

sheep

puppy

lamb

chipmunk

calf

cow

alligator

rabbit

butterfly

horse

pig

turtle

deer

beaver

skunk

lion

fawn

giraffe

tiger

elephant

kangaroo

ape

squirrel

camel

bear

fox

frog

tadpole

rhinoceros

mouse

zebra

kid   goat

ostrich

owl

hippopotamus

snake

lizard

fish

These are **animals**.

7

another

Here is a Teddy bear.
Here is **another** Teddy bear.

2. The boys and girls are playing
   with one **another**.

answer

1. The teacher asks a question.
   The children tell her the **answer**.
2. "Where are you going?" asks Sue.
   "I'm going home," Ann **answers**.

   answers   answered   answering

any

Are there **any** biscuits left?
No, there are not **any**.

anything

Is there **anything** in the cupboard?
No. There is nothing in the cupboard.

apple

An **apple** is a fruit.

arm

An **arm** is a part of the body.
Joe rests his **arms** on the **arms** of the chair.

army

The **army** has soldiers,
guns, and tanks.
Our **army** keeps us safe.

around

The children are running
around the tree.

as

1. Tom ran **as** fast **as** he could.
   He could not run any faster.

2. Betty went to the party **as** a fairy.
   Betty went dressed like a fairy.

ask

"**Ask** your mother if you may come."
"**I asked** her. She said I may."

   asks   asked   asking

asleep

Jenny is **asleep**.

at

Lorem ipsum

John is **at** the top of the ladder.
Ethel is **at** the bottom of the ladder.

autumn

The leaves fall from
the trees in the **autumn.**

awake

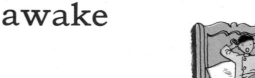

Bob is **awake**.
He is not asleep.

away

Father went **away** in an aircraft.
The cat ran **away** from the dog.

axe

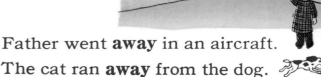

An **axe** is for chopping wood.

B b

The second letter in the alphabet

baboon

A **baboon** is an animal.

baby

Our **baby** is four weeks old.

back

1. Tim carries his books on his **back**.

2. The garden is at the **back** of the house.

3. Jo stands at the **back** of the class.

4. They ran to the gate and **back**.

5. Pat gives the toy
   back to the baby.

6. Mother is **backing** the car through the gate.

    backs   backed   backing

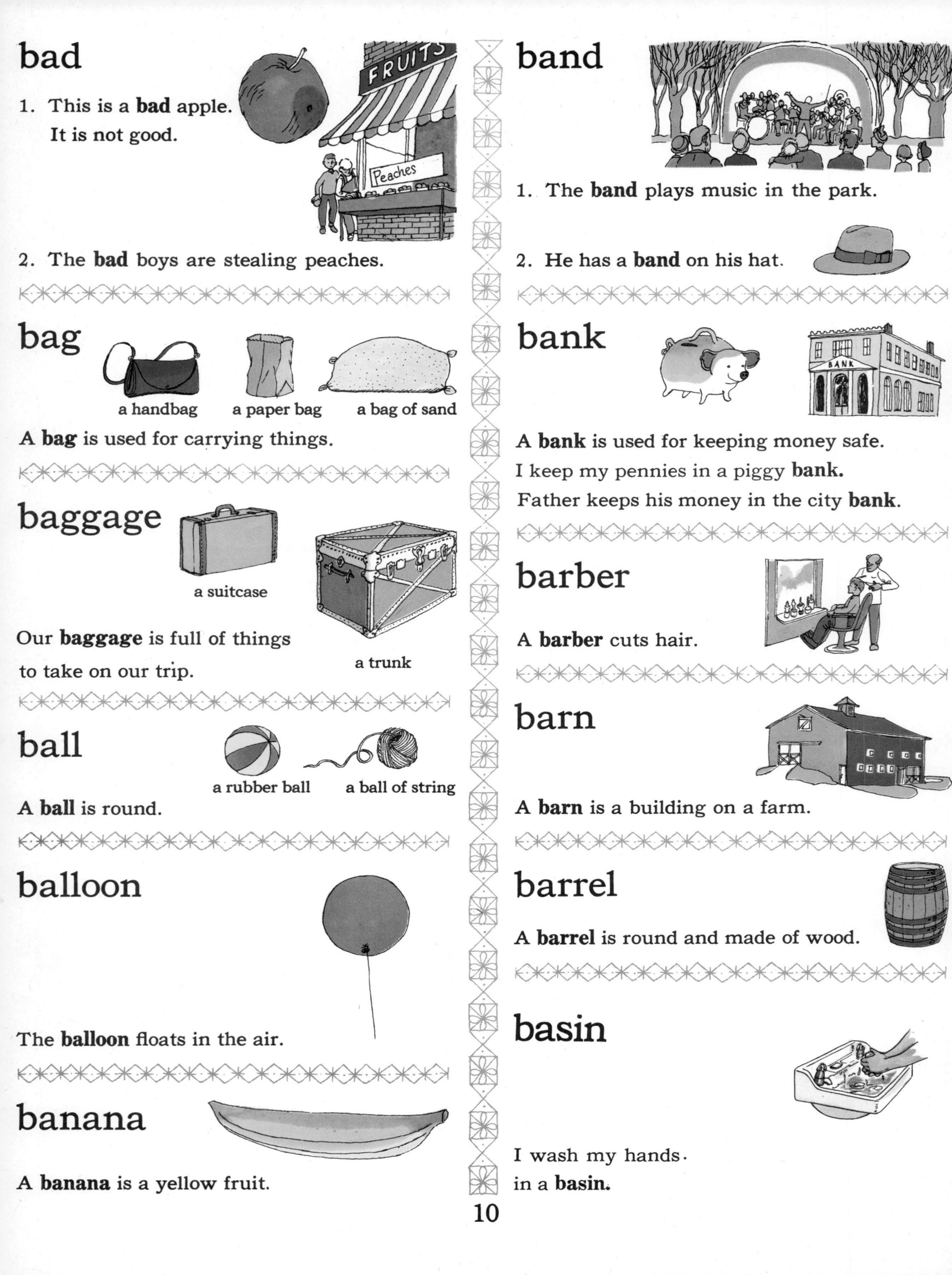

bad

1. This is a **bad** apple.
   It is not good.

2. The **bad** boys are stealing peaches.

bag

a handbag   a paper bag   a bag of sand

A **bag** is used for carrying things.

baggage

a suitcase

a trunk

Our **baggage** is full of things
to take on our trip.

ball

a rubber ball   a ball of string

A **ball** is round.

balloon

The **balloon** floats in the air.

banana

A **banana** is a yellow fruit.

band

1. The **band** plays music in the park.

2. He has a **band** on his hat.

bank

A **bank** is used for keeping money safe.
I keep my pennies in a piggy **bank.**
Father keeps his money in the city **bank.**

barber

A **barber** cuts hair.

barn

A **barn** is a building on a farm.

barrel

A **barrel** is round and made of wood.

basin

I wash my hands.
in a **basin.**

10

basket

an Easter basket   a market basket   a clothes basket

A **basket** is made of wood or twigs.

bat

Bruce has a **bat**.

He uses it to **bat** the ball.

bats   batted   batting

bat

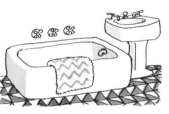

A **bat** is an animal that flies at night.

bath

A **bath** makes you clean.

We use the big **bath tub**.

The **bath tub** is in the **bathroom**.

be

Be a good boy.

I **am** going to school.

Patsy **is** going to school.

We **will be** home at nine o'clock.

John and Henry **are** going, too.

Yesterday I **was** late.

John and Henry **were** early.

Today we **have been** hurrying.

We want to **be** early.

We **shall be** early.

am   is   was   were   been   being

bead

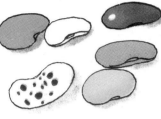

Beads are strung on a string.

bean

A **bean** is a vegetable.

Beans are good to eat.

bear

A **bear** is an animal with a thick fur coat.

There are white **bears**, brown **bears**,

and black **bears**.

beautiful

Beautiful things are nice to look at.

Beautiful music is pleasing to hear.

because

Paula's plant died **because** she did not water it.

bed

We go to sleep in a **bed**.

The **bed** is in the **bed**room.

bee

bumblebee   honeybee

A **bee** makes honey.

before

1. Jack stood **before** Jane.
2. We wash our hands **before** each meal.

begin

We **begin** to write at the top of the page.

begins   began   beginning

behind

Harold is **behind** the door.

believe

Do you **believe** in fairies?

Do you think there are fairies?

believes   believed   believing

bell

  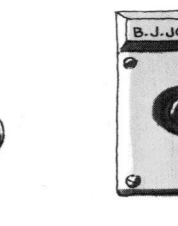    

1. The school **bell** rings in the morning.
2. The church **bells** ring on Sunday.
3. Mary rings the **doorbell**.

belong

Does this **belong** to you?

Is this yours?

belongs   belonged   belonging

below

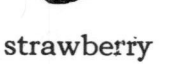

1. The little picture is **below** the big picture.
2. My mark was **below** ninety.
   My mark was less than ninety.

belt

A **belt** is a strip of leather or cloth.

1. A **belt** is worn around the waist.

machine belt

2. A **belt** turns a wheel on the machine.

bend

A **bend** is a curve.

1. The strong man made a **bend** in the iron bar.

2. John **bends** to pick up the ball.

bends   bent   bending

berry

raspberry   strawberry

A **berry** is a small fruit.

beside

Paula sits **beside** John.

best

This is a good apple.

This is a better apple.

This is the **best** apple.

between

Mary is **between** Tom and Bill.

Bible

In Sunday school we read the **Bible.**

bicycle

A **bicycle** has two wheels.
Walter is riding his **bicycle**.

big

The store building is **big**.
It is **bigger** than the house.
The bank building is the **biggest** of all.

bigger   biggest

bird

A **bird** is an animal with feathers.

turkey

pigeon

crow

chicken

canary

robin

sparrow

humming-bird

woodpecker

eagle

parrot

owl

penguin

guinea-hen

bluebird

ostrich

sea-gull

goose

duck

stork

pelican

wild duck

These are birds.

13

bite

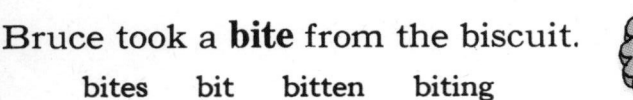

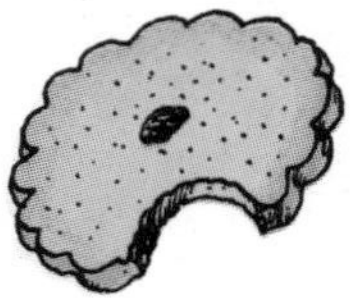

Bruce took a **bite** from the biscuit.

bites   bit   bitten   biting

bitter

Bitter things do not taste good.

black

Black is a colour.

blackboard

The teacher writes on the **blackboard**.

blade

1. We cut with the **blade** of the knife.
2. Here is a **blade** of grass.

blind

The **blind** man cannot see.

block

1. Bruce is building with his **blocks**.
2. The lorry **blocked** the road. 

blocks   blocked   blocking

blue

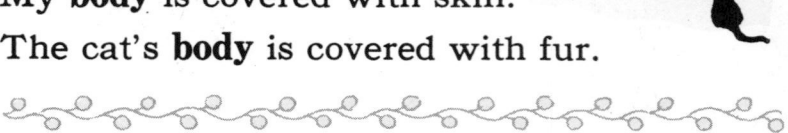

Blue is a colour.

board

A **board** is a long flat piece of wood.

boat

a rowing boat   a steamboat   a sailing boat

We crossed the lake in a **boat**.

body

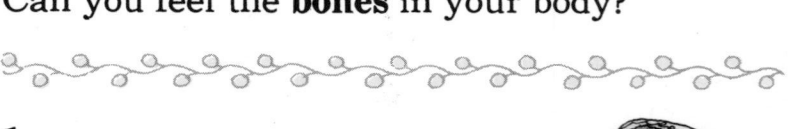

My **body** is covered with skin.
The cat's **body** is covered with fur.

bone

These are the **bones** of a fish.
Bob gives Rover a **bone**.
Can you feel the **bones** in your body?

bonnet

The baby has a blue **bonnet**.

book

A **book** has many printed pages.
This is a **book**.

14

both

Both my hands are full.

bottle

a milk bottle

a medicine bottle

A **bottle** is made of glass and has a little neck. **Bottles** hold liquids.

bottom

The mat is at the **bottom** of the stairs.

bow

1. Sue has a pink **bow** in her hair.

2. Jack has a **bow** and arrow.

bowl

A **bowl** is a deep dish.

box

a jack-in-the-box

boxes

We keep things in **boxes.**

boy

Tom is a **boy.**

branch

1. A **branch** fell off the tree.
2. The road **branches** off the highway.

brave

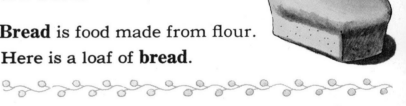

Jim was **brave** in the dentist's chair. He did not cry or make a fuss.

bread

Bread is food made from flour. Here is a loaf of **bread.**

break

Did Anne **break** her doll?
breaks   broke   broken   breaking

breakfast

Breakfast is the first meal of the day.

breath

Take a deep **breath** through your nose. **Breathe** through your nose.
breathes   breathed   breathing

15

bridge

The **bridge** spans the river.

bright

The **bright** sun gets in my eyes.

broom

A **broom** is used to sweep the floor.

brother

Tom is my **brother**.
We have the same father and mother.

brush

a clothes brush   a scrubbing brush

a paint brush   a tooth brush

Brushes are used for cleaning or painting.

bud

The **bud** will open
into a leaf or flower.

build

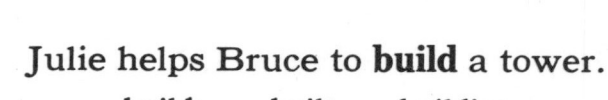

Julie helps Bruce to **build** a tower.

builds   built   building

building

Houses, churches, and schools
are **buildings**.
These are **buildings**.

bulb

1. This **bulb** will grow into a tulip.

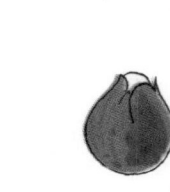

2. The electric light **bulb** lights
   the room at night.
   The light **bulb** is the same shape
   as the tulip **bulb**.

bun

Judy made some **buns.**

burn

1. Fire **burns**.
2. Joe has a **burn** on his wrist.

burns   burned   burnt   burning

bus

We ride to school in a **bus.**

but

1. Steve pulled hard
   but the donkey would not come.

2. I ate all **but** the bones.
   I did not eat the bones.

butcher

The **butcher** sells meat.

butter

Butter is food.
It is made from cream.

C c

The third letter in the alphabet

cage

We keep our canary in a **cage.**
He cannot fly away.

button

Buttons are used to fasten clothing.
Jane fastened the **buttons**
on her coat.

a coat button

buy

Helen had a shiny coin.
She took it to **buy** sweets.

buys   bought   buying

by

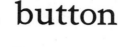

1. The tree is **by** the fence.

2. The lorry went **by** the house.

3. The cart was pulled **by** the horse.

4. They went to town **by** train.

cake

A **cake** is sweet and good to eat.
Mother has baked a **cake**.

call

1. Henry makes a telephone **call**.
2. Jean is **calling** the kitten.

calls   called   calling

17

camera

Mother is taking our pictures with a **camera**.

can

"**Can** you reach the box?"
"I **could** if you would lift me up."

can   could

can

a can of fruit   an oil can

We keep things in tin **cans**.

candle

A **candle** gives a little light.
The **candle** is made of wax or tallow.

canoe

The redskin paddles his **canoe.**

cap

a nurse's cap   a hunter's cap   a bottle cap

A **cap** is a small hat or cover.

car

This is a **car.**
We can ride in a **car.**

card

A **card** is a stiff piece of paper.
1. Ruth got a post **card**.

2. We play games with **cards**.

care

Ann takes **care** of the baby.
Tom always crosses streets with **care**.

carry

The girls **carry** their dolls.
carries   carried   carrying

castle

A **castle** is a very big house.
King Arthur lived in a **castle**.

cat

A **cat** is an animal with fur.
Our **cat** catches mice.

catch

1. Ruth will **catch** the ball.

2. Ben is trying to **catch** up with Sue.
catches   caught   catching

18

centipede

Centipedes have many legs.

centre

The hole is in the **centre** of the doughnut.
The hole is in the middle of the doughnut.

cereal

Cereal is made of grain.
We eat **cereal** for breakfast.

chain

Chains are made of links.

chair

straight chair   rocking chair   high chair

We sit on **chairs**.

chalk

We write on the blackboard with **chalk**.

change

1. Patsy and Tom **change** places.

2. I gave fivepence for a twopence biscuit.
   The grocer gave me threepence **change.**

   changes   changed   changing

cheese

Cheese is food made from milk.

chest

1. The **chest** is a part of the body.
   The soldier wears a medal on his **chest**.

2. A **chest** is a piece of furniture.

   We keep our clothes in a **chest**.

chick

A **chick** is a baby bird.
The **chick** has just hatched from an egg.

chicken

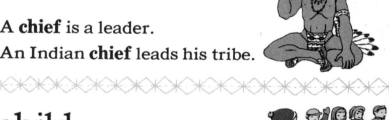

Jim feeds the **chickens**.
We eat **chicken** for food.

chief

A **chief** is a leader.
An Indian **chief** leads his tribe.

child

Sammy is a **child**.
Boys and girls are **children**.

chin

The **chin** is a part of the face.
Betty has paint on her **chin**.

19

choose

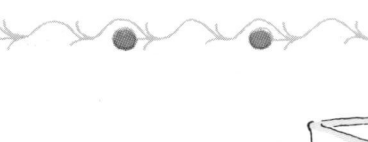

Tom may **choose** either biscuit.
Which will he **choose**?

chooses   chose   chosen   choosing

Christmas

Christmas is Jesus Christ's birthday.
Christmas is December 25th.

circle

A **circle** is round.
Jerry drew a **circle**.

circus

A **circus** has trained animals and funny clowns.

city

A **city** has many buildings and houses.
Many people live in **cities**.

class

These children are in a **class** in school.

clean

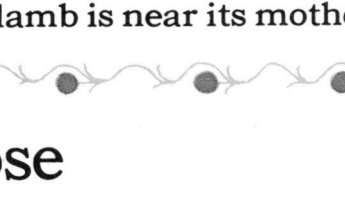

Mary's hands are **clean**.
She has washed off the dirt.

cleans   cleaned   cleaning

clear

The water is **clear** and
we can see the fish.

climb

Bill **climbs** the ladder.

climbs   climbed   climbing

clock

We tell time by the **clock**.

close

The lamb is **close** to its mother.
The lamb is near its mother.

close

Tom will **close** the door.

closes   closed   closing

cloth

Cloth is woven from threads.
Jane's dress is made of **cloth**.

clothes

We wear **clothes**.
This is **clothing**.

panties

pinafore

stockings

hat

bonnet

coat

socks

nightdress

sweater

overcoat

scarf

raincoat

bib

pyjamas

skirt

trousers

shirt

dress

mittens

shoes

slip

bathing suit

overalls

snow suit

cap

boots

---

cloud

Clouds float in the sky.

clown

A **clown** is a funny man in the circus.

coal

a lump of coal

a coal mine

Coal is dug from the ground.
Coal burns and makes heat.

coat

raincoat

overcoat

A **coat** is a covering.

1. We wear a **coat** over other clothes.

2. A rabbit has a **coat** of fur.

3. The painter puts a **coat** of paint on the wall.

cold

1. **Cold** weather comes in winter.
2. Ralph has a **cold** in his nose.

collar

a man's collar

a lace collar

a dog's collar

A **collar** is worn around the neck.

21

colour

These are **colours**.

red	orange	yellow	green	blue
purple	black	white	brown	pink	grey

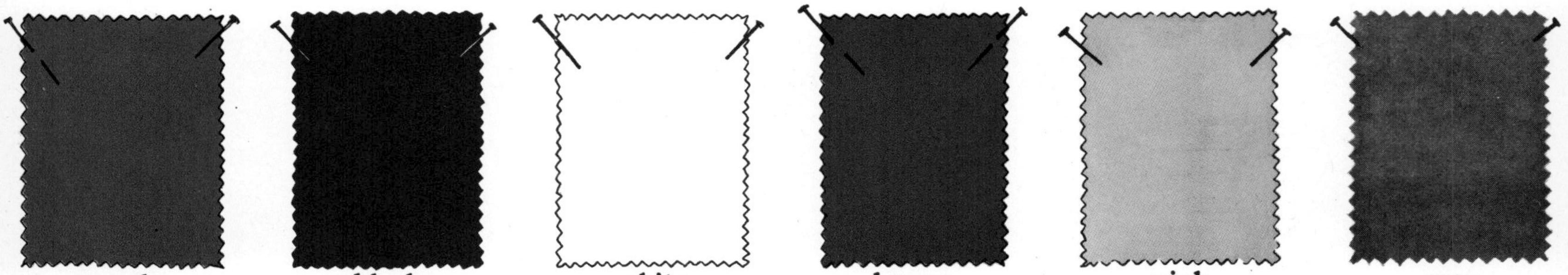

comb

We use a **comb** to **comb** our hair.

   combs   combed   combing

come

"**Come**, Rover! **Come** here!"
Rover **comes** to Jim.

   comes   came   coming

cook

1. The **cook** wears a
   tall, white cap.

2. Sue helps mother to **cook** dinner.

   cooks   cooked   cooking

cool

Cool means not very cold.
A **cool** drink is good in summer.

copy

Teacher said, "**Copy** your lesson."
We made a **copy** of our lesson
from the blackboard.

   copies   copied   copying

corn

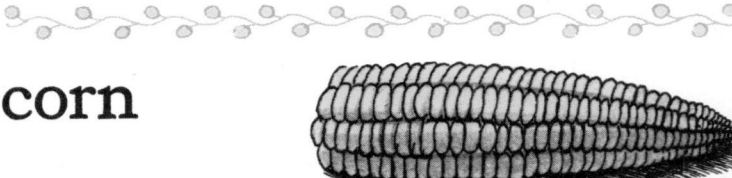

Corn is a grain.
This is a **corn**-cob.

corner

Angus sits in the **corner**.

cost

"How much does the biscuit **cost**?"

"It **costs** fivepence."

costs   cost   costing

cough

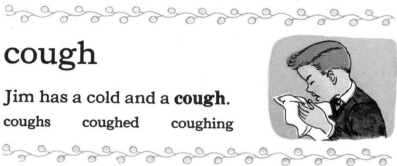

Jim has a cold and a **cough**.

coughs   coughed   coughing

count

We **count** the chickens.

"One, two, three, four, five."

counts   counted   counting

country

1. Farms and woods are in the **country**.
2. England is a **country**.
   America is another **country**.

cousin

Your **cousin** is a child
of your aunt or uncle.

cover

Saucepan cover   box cover   bed covers

We put **covers** over things.

The saucepan is **covered**.

covers   covered   covering

cow

A **cow** is an animal.

She gives us milk.

crack

There is a **crack** in the cup.

Who **cracked** the cup?

cracks   cracked   cracking

cracker

I pull the **cracker** with my sister.

cradle

A **cradle** is a baby's bed.

Jane rocks the baby in the **cradle**.

crayon

We draw with coloured **crayons**.

cross

1. Jack drew a red **cross** on the board.
2. The baby is **cross**. He is crying.

cry

We **cry** when we are unhappy.

cries   cried   crying

cup

I have a **cup** of milk.

cupboard

The **cupboard** is full.

curl

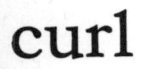

The pig has a **curl** in its tail.
Mary's mother **curls** her hair.

curls   curled   curling

cut

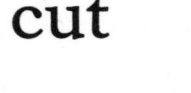

1. Susan **cut** her finger.

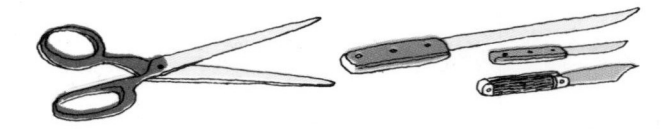

2. Scissors and knives are for **cutting**.

cuts   cut   cutting

D d

The fourth letter of the alphabet

daddy

I call my father "**Daddy**."

dance

We **dance** to the music.

dances   danced   dancing

danger

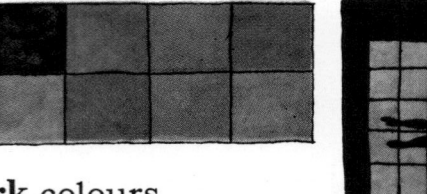

The sign says **Danger**.
We must be careful.

dark

1. These are **dark** colours.

2. We cannot see in the **dark.**

daughter

A girl is a **daughter** of her mother and father.

day

1. The **day** comes after the night.
2. The seven **days** of the week are Monday,
   Tuesday, Wednesday, Thursday,
   Friday, Saturday, and Sunday.

dead

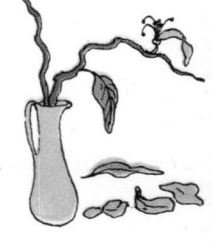

Dead means not living any more.
The flower is **dead**.

deep

We dug a **deep** hole in the ground.

dentist

A **dentist** takes care of our teeth.

24

desk

A **desk** holds papers and pencils.
Helen keeps her **desk** tidy.

destroy

The storm **destroys** the bridge.
It is broken to pieces.

destroys   destroyed   destroying

dictionary

A **dictionary** tells what words mean.
This book is a **dictionary.**

different

These flowers are **different.**
These flowers are not alike.

dig

I **dig** a hole with my spade.

digs   dug   digging

dim

The light is **dim.**
The light is not bright.

dinner

Dinner is the biggest meal of the day.

direction

1. **Directions** explain what to do.

2. The signpost points the **direction.**
   It shows where to go.

dirt

Sam digs in the **dirt**.
His overalls are **dirty**.

dish

The **dish** is blue.
Our meals are served in **dishes.**

distance

The farm is a long **distance**
from the town.
The farm is far from the town.

divide

Mother will **divide** the pie.
Mother will cut the pie into pieces.

divides   divided   dividing

do

1. **Do** you see an aircraft?
   Can you see an aircraft?
2. **Did** you **do** your work?
   Have you finished your work?
3. How **do** you **do?**
   How are you?

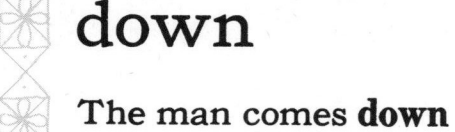

does   did   doing

doctor

The **doctor** takes care of us
when we are sick.

dog

A **dog** is an animal.
Dogs make good pets.

doll

A **doll** is a toy.
Ruth's **doll** is dressed like a baby.

donkey

A **donkey** is an animal.
We go for **donkey** rides at the seaside.

door

The **door** is open.

down

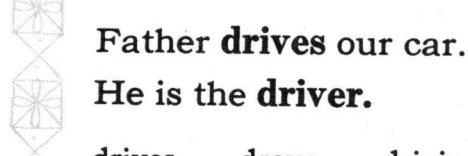

The man comes **down**
in a parachute.

draw

1. The horse **draws** the cart.
   The horse pulls the cart.

2. Bill likes to **draw** pictures.

draws   drew   drawing

dream

Sometimes we **dream** of things
while we are sleeping.
Can you remember what you **dream?**

dreams   dreamed   dreaming

dress

Patsy has a yellow **dress.**
Girls and women wear **dresses.**

drink

Jim takes a **drink** of milk.
He is **drinking** a glass of milk.

drinks   drank   drinking

drive

Father **drives** our car.
He is the **driver.**

drives   drove   driving

drop

A **drop** of rain **dropped**
on the window sill.

    drops   dropped   dropping

drum

We beat a **drum** with **drumsticks**.

dry

The wet clothes will soon be **dry**.
The clothes are **drying** on the line.

    dries   dried   drying

duck

Ducks are birds that live
near water.
They swim and fly.

during

During the shower we stayed indoors.
While it was raining we stayed indoors.

dust

Mother **dusts** the chair.
She takes off the **dust**
with a **duster.**

    dusts   dusted   dusting

E e

The fifth letter of the alphabet

each

There is a spoon on **each** plate.
There is a spoon on every plate.

ear

1. Our **ears** are for hearing.

2. An **ear** of corn
   grows on the stalk.

early

The cock crows **early** in the morning.
It crows before we get up.

earth

1. We plant seeds in the **earth.**

2. The world is called the **Earth.**

east

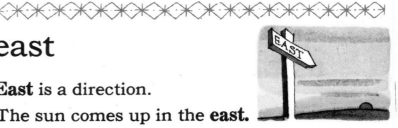

East is a direction.
The sun comes up in the **east.**

27

easy

It is **easy** to slide down.
It is not **easy** to climb up.

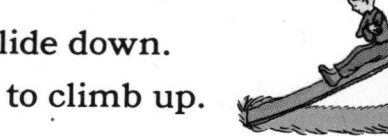

eat

We **eat** our food.
Last night we **ate** chicken.

eats   ate   eaten   eating

edge

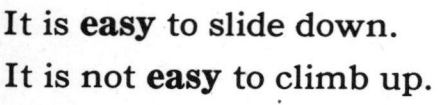

The handkerchief has a lace **edge.**

egg

A bird's **egg** is in the nest.
We eat hens' **eggs.**

eight

8

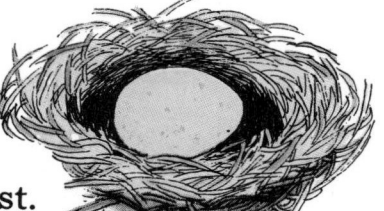

Eight is a number.
Here are **eight** candles.

either

Sam may take **either** the big book
or the little book.
He may have one or the other.

electric

We have **electric** lights,
an **electric** iron,
and an **electric** fan.

else

1. "Will you take anything **else?**"
   "Will you take anything more?"
2. "Who **else** will play on our side?"
   "We need one more player."

empty

The pail is **empty.**
The pail has nothing in it.

end

Ruth is at the **end** of the line.
She is the last one in the line.

engine

1. This **engine** pulls the train.
2. A car has an **engine.**

enjoy

We **enjoy** playing in the sand.
We like to play in the sand.

enjoys   enjoyed   enjoying

enough

There is not **enough** ribbon
to go round the package.

Tom is tall **enough** to reach the shelf.

enter

We **enter** the church quietly.
We go into the church quietly.

envelope

A letter is in the **envelope.**

equal

The pie is cut in **equal** parts.
Each piece is the same size.

error

$$2 + 2 = 5$$

Peter said that two and two make five.
Peter made an **error.**

$$2 + 2 = 4$$

even

1. The dog runs **even** when he is tired.

2. Jane folds the cloth so that
   the edges are **even.**

evening

Evening is the end of the day.
In the **evening** it grows dark.

ever

"Were you **ever** late?"
"No. I was never late."

every

Every dog has a tail.
All dogs have tails.

everything

Did you eat **everything**
that was on your plate?

except

All the children went to school
except the baby.
All the children went to school,
but not the baby.

expect

We **expect** to see the circus.
We think that we shall see the circus.

   expects   expected   expecting

eye

1. We see with our **eyes.**

2. Thread goes through the **eye**
   of a needle.

F f

The sixth letter of the alphabet

face

Timothy has a smiling **face.**

fact

A **fact** is something we know.
Two and two makes four.
This is a **fact.**

fair

Johnny is a **fair** player.
Johnny is an honest player.

fair

The Third Little Pig
went to the **fair.**

fairy

Jane believes in **fairies.**

Do you like to hear
fairy tales?

fall

Sam is going to **fall.**
Whoops! There he goes down.

falls   fell   fallen   falling

false

False means not true.
It is **false** to say that the sun rises
in the evening.

family

Parents and children make a **family.**
The **family** is out walking.

fan

A **fan** is used to keep us cool.

far

The school is near the house.
The church is **far** from the house.
The bank is **farther** away.
The store is **farthest** from the house.

farm

Farmer Brown lives on a **farm.**
Farmers grow food for us to eat.
They grow vegetables, fruit, and cereals.

fast

Bob ran **fast**.
He won the race.

fat

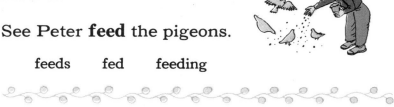

The pink pig is **fat**.
The black pig is not **fat**.

father

Father is head of the family.

feather

Birds are covered with **feathers**.

feed

See Peter **feed** the pigeons.

feeds   fed   feeding

feel

1. Jane **feels** the cat's soft fur.

2. Bob is not **feeling** well.
   He is sick.

feels   felt   feeling

fence

The **fence** goes around
the front garden.

few

There are a **few** eggs in the nest.
There are not many eggs in the nest.

field

The **field** has trees at the edges.

fifteen   **15**

Fifteen is a number.
Ten and five make **fifteen**.
10 and 5 make **15**.

fifty   **50**

Fifty is a number.
Five tens make **fifty**. $5 \times 10 = 50$
5 tens make **50**.

fight

A soldier **fights**.

fights   fought   fighting

figure

1. We write numbers with **figures**.
2. The girl is **figure** skating.

fill

I **fill** the pail full of water.

fills   filled   filling

31

find

Judy cannot **find** her shoe.
She has looked for it everywhere.

finds   found   finding

finger

A **finger** is a part of the hand.
Bill points with his **finger.**

finish

Mother read us part of a story.
Today she will **finish** it.

finishes   finished   finishing

fire

A **fire** burns and gives
light and heat.
We made a little **fire.**

first

Mary sits in the **first** seat.
A is the **first** letter of the alphabet.

fish

1. **Fish** live in the water.
2. These boys are **fishing**.

fishes   fished   fishing

five 5

Five is a number.
Here are **five** little pigs.

fix

Patsy broke her doll.
Father will **fix** it.

fixes   fixed   fixing

flag

The **flag** blows in the wind.
It is the **flag** of Great Britain.

flame

A **flame** is bright and hot.
The lighted match makes a **flame.**

flat

The roof is **flat**.

float

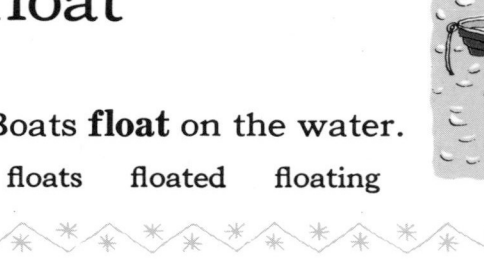

Boats **float** on the water.

floats   floated   floating

floor

The rug is on the **floor.**

flour

Mother made a cake.
She used **flour.**
Flour is made from wheat.

32

flower

Flowers grow on plants.
These are **flowers**.

geranium

carnation

daisy

daffodil

petunia

tulip

lily

violet

pansy

rose

orchid

poppy

gardenia

buttercup

lily-of-the-valley

dog-rose

ladyslipper

jack-in-the-pulpit

lilac

apple blossom

chrysanthemum

fly

1. A **fly** is an insect which can **fly**.

2. Birds and aircraft can **fly**.

flies   flew   flown   flying

fold

Can you **fold** a handkerchief?

folds   folded   folding

follow

The kitten **follows** its mother.
The kitten comes after its mother.

follows   followed   following

food

We eat **food**.
Here is some **food**.

chop

roast beef

sausages

chicken

cake   bread   butter   celery

lettuce

eggs

fish

nuts

carrots

sugar

beans

cheese

grapes

biscuits

potato

tomato

ice cream

milk

soup

pie

apple

33

foot

1. The **foot** is a part of the body.
   Each **foot** has five toes.
   We stand on our two **feet.**

2. The rug is at the **foot**
   of the stairs.

for

1. It is a good day **for** a picnic.
   It is a good day to go on a picnic.
2. I gave twopence **for** a biscuit.
   I bought a biscuit with my pocket-money.
3. I washed the dishes **for** mother.
   She did not have to do them.
4. Bill is looking **for** his hat.
   He wants to find his hat.
5. Get ready **for** bed!
   Get ready to go to bed!

forest

Red Riding Hood went
into the **forest.**
Many trees make a **forest.**

fork

I eat with a **fork**.

four

Four is a number.
There are **four** marbles.

fox

A **fox** is an animal.
The **fox** met the gingerbread boy.

free

1. We let the bird go **free.**
   The bird can do what it likes.

2. The sweets they gave us
   were **free.**
   We didn't have to pay for them.

friend

Helen and Grace are **friends.**
They like each other.

from

1. Rover runs **from** Ann to Bob.
   He runs to Bob **from** Ann.
2. Smoke is coming **from** the chimney.
   Smoke is coming out of the chimney.
3. **From** that day they lived happily.
   After that day they lived happily.
4. Books are made **from** paper.
   Books are made of paper.

front

A coat opens down the **front.**

Mary ran in the **front** door.

fruit

Many **fruits** are good to eat.
<u>These are **fruits.**</u>

banana

orange

pineapple

cherries

strawberries

cantaloup

apple

lemon

plum

raspberry

peach

pear

gooseberry

bilberries

grapefruit

grapes

watermelon

full

The basket is **full.**
It has many groceries in it.

fun

The children are having **fun.**
They like to play.

funny

The **funny** clown made us laugh.

fur

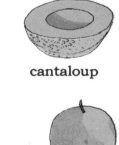

Some animals have coats of **fur.**

furniture

We have **furniture** in the house.
<u>This is **furniture**.</u>

lamp

bed

arm-chair

straight chair

desk

stool

table

clock

sideboard

rocking chair

carpet

mirror

bureau

bookcase

sofa

G g

The seventh letter of the alphabet

game

The boys are playing a **game.**

garage

We keep the car in the **garage.**

garden

Plants and flowers grow in the **garden.**

gas

We have a **gas** stove for cooking.

gay

1. **Gay** colours are bright.
2. John is **gay** today.
   He is happy.

gate

A **gate** is a doorway
in a fence or wall.

get

1. Judy will **get** the biscuits.
2. Our feet **got** cold in the snow.
3. Are the children **getting** up?
4. Henry **got** a letter.

gets got getting

giant

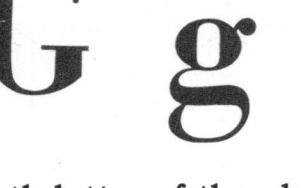

Jack met a **giant**.
The **giant** was a very big man.

gift

Santa Claus gave Mary Ellen
a **gift**.

girl

Jane is a **girl**.

give

Mother **gives** Bob a gift.

gives gave given giving

glad

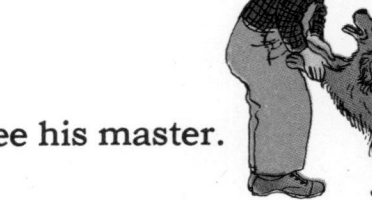

The dog is **glad** to see his master.
He is very happy.

36

glass

1. Windows are made of **glass.**

2. We drink from a **glass.**

3. Grandmother wears **glasses** to help her see better.

glove

We wear **gloves** on our hands.

go

Edith will **go** to the store.

goes   went   gone   going

goat

A **goat** is an animal.
Goats give milk.

God

God is our Father in Heaven.

gold

1. **Gold** is a yellow-coloured metal.

2. Ann has **golden** curls.

good

1. Mary is a **good** girl.
   She helps her mother.
2. Biscuits are **good** to eat.
3. Biscuits taste **good.**

   better   best

good-bye

They are waving **good-bye.**

gradual

We bicycled up a **gradual** slope.
We bicycled up a slight hill.

grain

1. Wheat, corn, oats, and barley
   are **grain** plants.
   They are tall grasses.
   Grain is the seed of the **grain** plants.

2. Tom let the **grains** of sand fall
   through his hand.
   Grains of sand are like small seed **grains.**

3. The **grain** of wood is shown
   by the lines in it.

grandfather

I have two **grandfathers.**
One is my mother's father.
One is my father's father.

grandmother

I have two **grandmothers.**
One is my mother's mother.
One is my father's mother.

grape

Grapes are fruit.
They grow in bunches
on a vine.

grass

The **grass** covers the ground.

great

1. The **great** mountain is very high.
2. The **great**-grandmother is very old.
3. President Lincoln was a **great** man.

green

Green is a colour.
Grass is **green.**

grocer

The **grocer** sells things to eat.
The **grocer** sells **groceries.**

ground

Plants grow in the **ground.**

group

One star is by itself.
The others are in a **group.**

grow

My little rabbit will **grow.**
He will get bigger.

grows   grew   grown   growing

guess

Guess where Tim is hiding.
You may have two **guesses.**

guesses   guessed   guessing

guide

The **guide** takes us fishing.
He **guides** us up the river.

guides   guided   guiding

gun

Guns are used for shooting.

H h

The eighth letter of the alphabet

hair

We have **hair** on our heads.
A dog is covered with **hair.**

half

The pie is cut in **half.**
The two **halves** are the same size.

Hallowe'en

Hallowe'en is the last day
of October.
It is fun to dress as a witch
and carry a **Hallowe'en** lantern.

hammer

A **hammer** is used for hitting nails.

hand

1. My **hand** has four fingers
   and a thumb.

2. A clock has two **hands**
   that point to the time.

handkerchief

I carry a **handkerchief**
to wipe my nose.

handle

We hold things by the **handles.**

hang

The coat **hangs** on the hook.

hangs   hung   hanging

happen

What will **happen?**
What will take place?

happens   happened   happening

happy

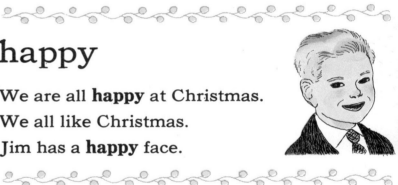

We are all **happy** at Christmas.
We all like Christmas.
Jim has a **happy** face.

hard

1. Stones are **hard.**
2. The farmer works **hard.**

hat

A **hat** is worn on the head.

have

I **have** a book in my hand.
I **had** a visitor last week.
has   had   having

hay

Hay is dried grass.
We feed **hay** to farm animals.
The farmer puts **hay** in a **hay**stack to dry.

he

Bill is a boy.
He is a boy.
his   him   himself

head

1. Tom has turned his **head.**

2. The pin has a green **head.**

3. Betty is at
   the **head** of the stairs.

health

When we are well, we are in good **health.**
When we are sick, we are in poor **health.**

hear

We **hear** with our ears.
hears   heard   hearing

heart

Our **hearts** beat in our bodies.
The Valentine is **heart**-shaped.

heat

Fire gives off **heat.**
Fire makes us warm.

heavy

The box is too **heavy** to lift.
It weighs too much to lift.

hello

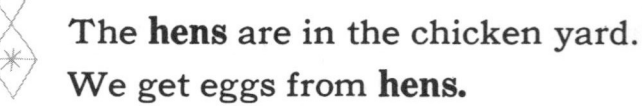

We say "**Hello**" when we meet someone.
Bill says "**Hello!**" to Mary.

help

Ann **helps** Mother with the dishes.
helps   helped   helping

hen

The **hens** are in the chicken yard.
We get eggs from **hens.**

here

"Come **here,** Rover," said Tom.
"Come to me, Rover."

hide

We are playing "**hide**-and-seek."
Where did Judy **hide?**
  hides   hid   hidden   hiding

high

The kite is **high** in the sky.

hill

The little **hill** is green.
Tom is running down the **hill**side.

hit

John **hit** the ball.
  hits   hit   hitting

hold

Alice **holds** the flower.
  holds   held   holding

hole

There is a **hole** in the coat.

holiday

A **holiday** is a special day of the year.
Christmas and Easter are **holidays.**

hollow

The squirrel lives
in a **hollow** tree.

home

Your **home** is where
you and your family live.

hook

1. I hang my clothes on a **hook.**
2. Father catches fish with a fish**hook.**

hoop

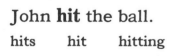

Tim rolls a **hoop.**

hop

George **hops** on one foot.
  hops   hopped   hopping

41

horn

1. The goat has **horns** on its head.

2. Peter blows the **horn.**

horse

A **horse** is a big animal.
We ride some **horses.**
Some **horses** pull carts.

hot

The water in the kettle is **hot.**

hour

Hours measure time.
There are 24 **hours** in a day.

house

A **house** is a building.
People live in **houses.**

how

1. **How** do you make it?
   In what way do you make it?
2. **How** far is it?
   What is the distance?
3. **How** are you?
   Are you well?

hundred

100

One **hundred** is a number.
Ten tens make one **hundred.**
10 tens make **100.**

hungry

Rover is **hungry.**
He wants his dinner.

hunt

1. The men are going to **hunt** a fox.
   The men are **hunters.**

2. I **hunt** for my lost book.
   hunts   hunted   hunting

hurry

Jack **hurries** to school.
If he goes slowly, he will be late.
   hurries   hurried   hurrying

hurt

Lassie has **hurt** her paw.
It pains her to walk on it.
   hurts   hurt   hurting

hut

The boys built a little **hut.**

I i

The ninth letter of the alphabet

I

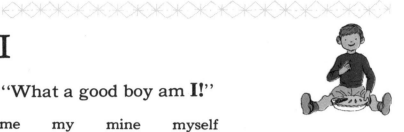

"What a good boy am **I**!"

me my mine myself

ice

Ice is frozen water.
Bill is skating on the **ice.**

There is **ice** in the refrigerator.

ice cream

Ice cream is good to eat.

if

1. **If** it rains, Ruth will put up the umbrella.
2. See **if** the door is locked.
   See whether the door is locked.

ill

Patsy is **ill.**
She is not well.

important

It is **important** to get
to school on time.

in

The baby is **in** the pram.

inch

An **inch** is a measure.
There are twelve **inches** in a foot.

Indian

Here is a Red **Indian.**
Red **Indians** live in America.
Indians live in India.

ink

We write with pen and **ink.**

insect

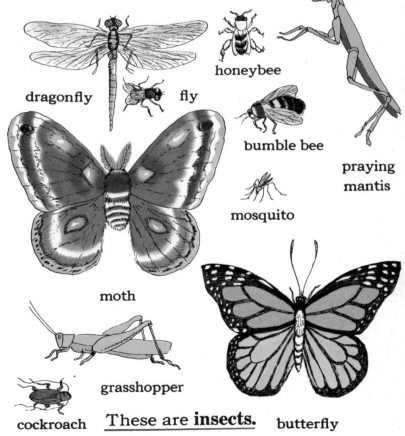

Insects are very small animals.

ant

honeybee

dragonfly fly

bumble bee

praying mantis

mosquito

moth

grasshopper

cockroach These are **insects.** butterfly

inside

John is **inside** the house.

instead

May I have milk **instead** of water?
May I have milk in place of water?

into

The rabbit went **into** his hole.

J j

The tenth letter of the alphabet

jacket

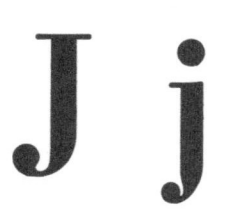

A **jacket** is a short coat.

jam

Jam is made from fruit and sugar.
We eat **jam** on bread.

jar

We put fruit in glass **jars**
to keep it all winter.

iron

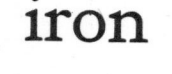

1. **Iron** is a strong metal.
2. Mother uses an electric **iron.**

island

An **island** is land
with water all around it.

it

1. I have a wagon. **It** is red.
2. **It** is fine today. The weather is fine today.

    its   itself

jelly

Jelly is made from fruit and sugar.
We eat **jelly** with ice cream.

jewel

A **jewel** is a bright and beautiful stone.

join

Join two pieces of string.
Tie two pieces of string together.

    joins   joined   joining

joke

A **joke** is a funny story.

joy

The dog was happy.
He wagged his tail with **joy.**

juice

We squeeze **juice** from fruit.
We drink orange **juice.**

jump

Sue likes to **jump** with a rope.

jumps   jumped   jumping

just

1. We have **just** enough milk
   to fill the glass.
   We have exactly enough milk
   to fill the glass.
2. The teacher is **just.**
   She is fair to us.

K k

The eleventh letter of the alphabet

keep

1. I **keep** my rabbit in a box.

2. George gave me a ball.
   I may **keep** it.

   keeps   kept   keeping

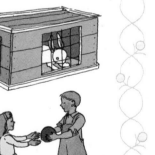

kettle

We heat water in a **kettle.**

key

We lock the door with a **key.**

kick

Ronald **kicks** the ball.

kicks   kicked   kicking

kindergarten

Little children go to **kindergarten.**
The **kindergarten** is in the school.

king

Some countries have a **king.**
He is the ruler of his country.
A **king** may wear a crown.

kiss

Tom's mother gives him a **kiss.**

kisses   kissed   kissing

kitchen

We cook in the **kitchen.**

kite

Jim flew his **kite** on a windy day.

kitten

A **kitten** is a young cat.
We call our **kitten** a kitty.

knee

Our legs bend at the **knee.**
John sits on his father's **knee.**

L l

The twelfth letter of the alphabet

lace

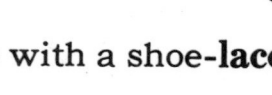

1. We use **lace** for trimming dresses.

2. Peter **laces** his shoe with a shoe-**lace.**

laces   laced   lacing

knife

A **knife** is for cutting.
We put **knives** and forks
on the table.

knock

Ann **knocks** at the door.
She **knocks** with the **knocker.**

knocks   knocked   knocking

knot

I tied a **knot** in the rope.

know

Do you **know** the answer?
Can you tell the answer?

knows   knew   knowing

ladder

We use a **ladder** for climbing.

lake

A **lake** is a large body of water
with land around it.

lamp

A **lamp** gives us light.

land

1. The farmer is ploughing his **land.**

2. Joe jumped from the wall. He **landed** on the grass.

lands   landed   landing

large

The eagle is a **large** bird.

last

1. John is the **last** to jump.
2. How long will the rain **last?**
   How long will the rain go on?

lasts   lasted   lasting

late

Peter is **late** for breakfast.
Everyone else is at the table.

laugh

We **laugh** at funny things.
We **laugh** when we are happy.

laughs   laughed   laughing

lawn

Grass grows on our **lawn.**

lay

1. Ruth **lays** her doll in the cradle.
2. The hen has **laid** an egg.

lays   laid   laying

lead

The man **leads** the horse.

Jim is the **leader** of the line.

leads   led   leading

leaf

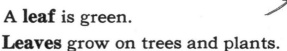

A **leaf** is green.
Leaves grow on trees and plants.

learn

Susie will **learn** how to sew.
Her mother is teaching her.

learns   learned   learning

leave

We **leave** our stockings for Santa.

Mother **left** the house.

leaves   left   leaving

left

1. I have two hands.
   One is my **left** hand.
   The other is my right hand.

2. Is there any ice cream **left?**
   Yes, there is still some ice cream.

leg

We stand on our **legs.**
Chairs also have **legs.**

length

What is the **length** of the board?
It is three feet long.

less

If I take one of your pears,
you will have one pear **less.**

let

1. We **let** the bird out of the cage.

2. Will you **let** me use your pencil?
   May I use your pencil?

   lets   let   letting

letter

1. There are 26 **letters** in
   the alphabet.
   L is a **letter.**

2. The **letter** came by mail.

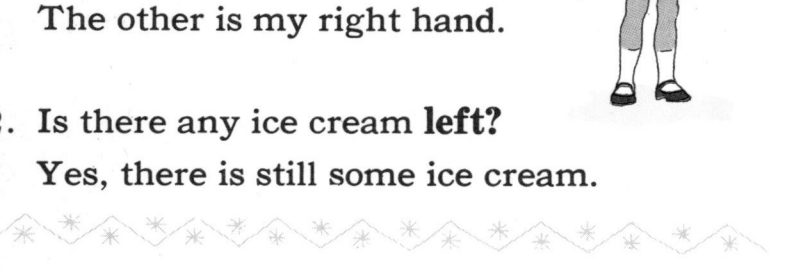

library

Books are kept in a **library.**

lid

1. We cover some things
   with **lids.**

2. Bruce's eye**lids** are closed.

lie

1. Harry did not tell the truth.
   He told a **lie.**

2. I **lie** in my bed and sleep.

   lies   lay   lain   lying

lift

The man will **lift** the ice.

   lifts   lifted   lifting

light

1. The sun gives **light.**

2. Ann's dress is a **light** colour.

3. The balloon is **light.**
   It floats in the air.

like

1. I **like** cats.
   I am fond of cats.

2. My cat looks **like** your cat.
   They look the same.

   likes   liked   liking

48

line

1. The clothes are on the clothes **line.**

2. The children wait in **line.**

3. John drew a red **line.**

lip

We have two **lips.**
We speak with our **lips.**

liquid

Water is **liquid.**
Oil is **liquid.**
There are many **liquids.**
We can pour **liquids.**

little

A mouse is a **little** animal.

live

The goldfish **live** in a bowl.

    lives   lived   living

long

The kite string is very **long.**
It is not short.

look

1. **Look** at the aircraft.
   See the aircraft.
2. I must **look** for my hat.
   I must search for my hat.

    looks   looked   looking

lose

Do not **lose** your mittens.
I am **lost.**
I do not know where I am.

    loses   lost   losing

loud

The lion gave a **loud** roar.
He made a great noise.

love

I **love** my dog.
I like him very much.

loves   loved   loving

low

The bookshelves are **low.**
I can reach them.

lunch

Lunch is a small meal.
I eat my **lunch** at noon.

Father takes a **lunch** box.

M m

The thirteenth letter of the alphabet

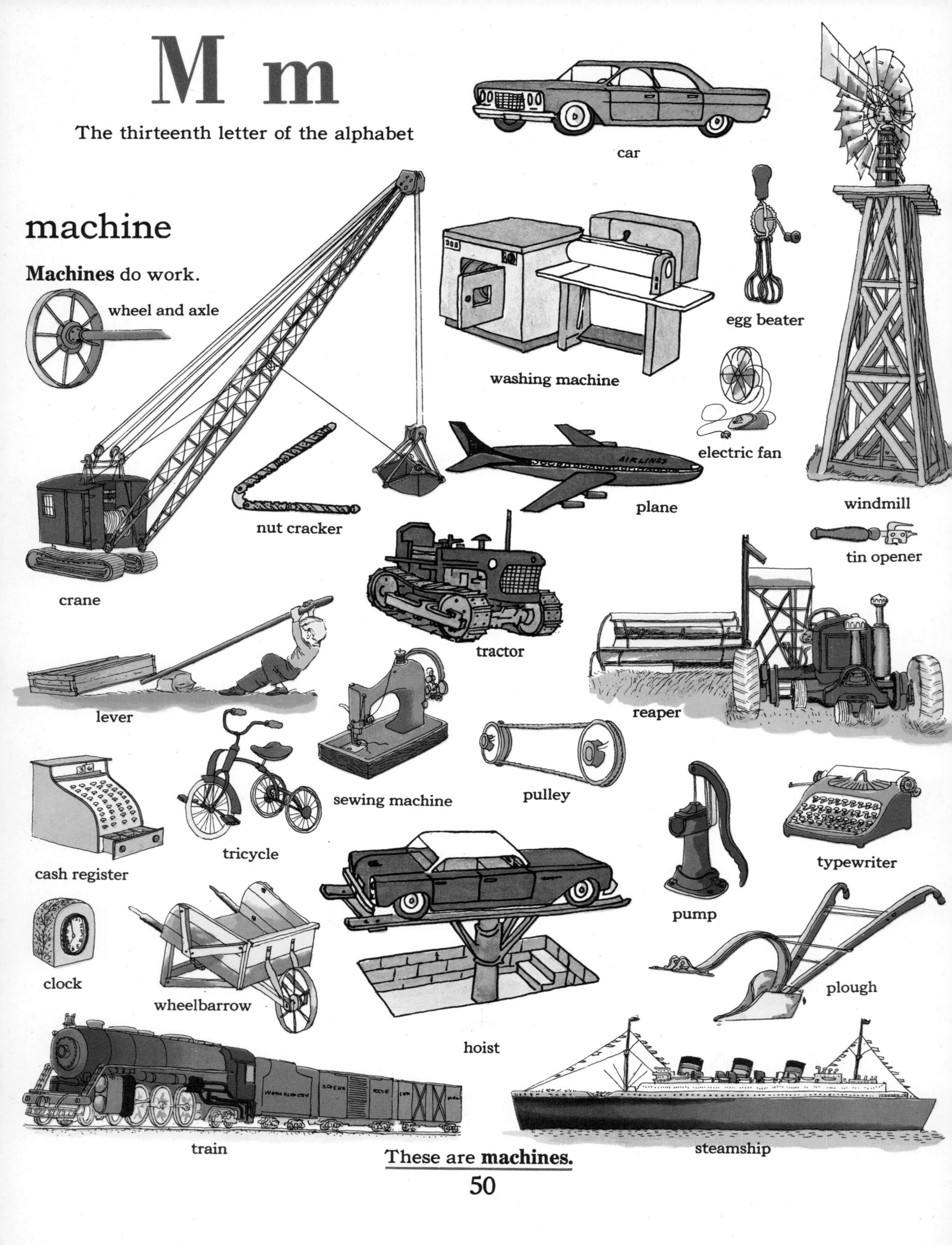

car

machine

Machines do work.

wheel and axle

washing machine

egg beater

electric fan

windmill

crane

nut cracker

plane

tin opener

tractor

reaper

lever

sewing machine

pulley

typewriter

cash register

tricycle

pump

clock

wheelbarrow

plough

hoist

train

steamship

These are **machines.**

50

mail

mailbag

We send letters and packages through the **mail.**

make

1. Mother will **make** a cake.
2. The bell **makes** a sound.
3. Two and two **make** four.

makes   made   making

man

Father is a **man.**
These are **men.**

many

1. How **many** marbles have you?
   What number of marbles have you?
2. I have **many** marbles.
   I have a lot of marbles

march

The schoolchildren **march** in line.

marches   marched   marching

mark

1. Lucy put a **mark** on the board.
2. We get **marks** on our report.
   They show how good our work is.

market

We go to the **market** to buy things.

match

1. We use a **match** to light a fire.

2. The two colours are a good **match.**
   They are alike.

may

1. "**May** I have a biscuit?"
   "Will you let me have a biscuit?"
2. Ralph **may** have a ball.
   Ask him if he has a ball.

might

meal

We have three **meals** a day.
We eat and drink at **meal**time.
Dinner is a **meal.**

measure

1. We will **measure** the ribbon
   to see how long it is.
2. An inch is a **measure** of length.

measures   measured   measuring

51

meat

We eat **meat**.

The butcher sells us **meat**.

chicken roast sausages chop

medicine

We take **medicine** when we are sick.

Medicine helps to make us well.

meet

Bill runs to **meet** his father.

meets   met   meeting

melt

The snow man **melts** in the sun.

melts   melted   melting

metal

Metal is found in the ground.

Gold and iron are **metals**.

These things are made of **metal**.

middle

1. Jane sits in the **middle** of the bench.

2. The hole is in the **middle** of the doughnut.

mile

A **mile** is a measure of distance.

It takes about twenty minutes

to walk a **mile**.

milk

We drink **milk**.

Cows give us **milk**.

The **milk**man brings the **milk**.

mill

1. Many things are made
   in **mills**.

   Flour is ground in a **mill**.

   The **miller** grinds the flour.

2. A wind**mill** is turned by the wind.

   It is used to pump water.

mind

1. We think in our **minds**.

2. Will you **mind** the baby?

   Will you watch her?

minds   minded   minding

minute

A **minute** is a measure of time.

It takes about a **minute** to count up to 60.

miss

We **miss** our dog.

He ran away.

We keep thinking of him.

misses   missed   missing

mistake

A **mistake** is something wrong.
Tom said two and two make five.
Tom made a **mistake.**

mitten

We wear **mittens** on our hands
to keep them warm.

mix

1. The alphabet blocks are **mixed** up.
   They are not in order.

2. Sue and Ted **mix** sand and
   water to make mud pies.

   mixes   mixed   mixing

money

We use **money** to buy things.

monkey

Monkeys are animals.
They climb trees.

month

A **month** is a measure of time.
There are 12 **months** in a year.
They are January, February, March, April,
May, June, July, August, September,
October, November, and December.

moon

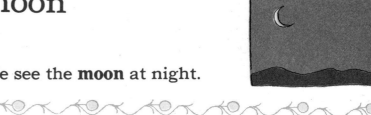

We see the **moon** at night.

more

Will you have some **more** soup?
Will you have another helping of soup?

morning

Morning is the first part of the day.
We get up in the **morning.**

most

Alice has more ice cream than Bruce.
John has the **most** ice cream.
John has more than Bruce or Alice.

mother

The **mother** loves her baby.
I live with my **mother** and father.

mountain

The **mountain** is bigger
than the hills.

mouse

A **mouse** is a small animal.
Mice like cheese.

mouth

Peter has his **mouth** open.

We eat and talk with our **mouths.**

move

1. I **move** my legs when I run.
2. We **moved** to a new town last week.
   We went to live in a new town.

    moves   moved   moving

much

1. How **much** cake is there?
   How many pieces of cake are there?
2. I have **much** work to do.
   I have a great deal of work to do.

N n

The fourteenth letter of the alphabet

nail

1. We join wood with **nails.**
   John drives a **nail** into the board.
2. We have **nails** at the ends
   of our fingers and toes.

name

We call each other by our **names.**

We know the **names** of many things.

mud

Mud is wet earth.

The rain makes the road **muddy.**

music

We like to hear **music.**

We sing and dance to **music.**

This is written **music.**

must

We **must** eat if we want to live and grow.

We have to eat if we want to live and grow.

narrow

The space is too **narrow**

for the pig to go through.

near

The dogs are **near** us.

The dogs are not far away.

neat

Mary keeps her desk **neat.**

Everything is in its right place.

neck

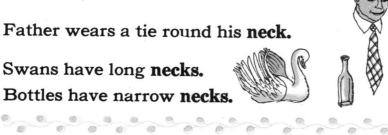

Father wears a tie round his **neck.**

Swans have long **necks.**
Bottles have narrow **necks.**

need

We **need** air to breathe.
We cannot live without air.

needs   needed   needing

needle

Jane sews with a **needle.**

neighbour

A **neighbour** is someone
who lives near you.

nest

Birds build **nests.**
They lay eggs and bring up
their young in **nests.**

net

1. Ruth has a **net** on her hair.

2. The fisherman catches fish in his **net.**

never

I am six years old.
I shall **never** be five again.
I shall not ever be five again.

new

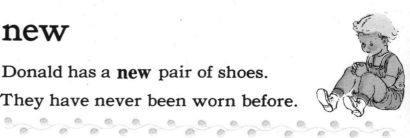

Donald has a **new** pair of shoes.
They have never been worn before.

news

What is the **news** today?
What new things have happened?

newspaper

We read news in the **newspaper.**
We get a **newspaper** every day.

next

1. Whose turn is **next?**
   Whose turn comes now?

2. Ann sat **next** to Mary.
   Ann sat beside Mary.

nice

We like **nice** things.
Ice cream is **nice** to eat.
New clothes are **nice** to wear.
Nice children behave well.

nickel

Nickel is a metal.
It looks like silver.

night

Night comes after the sun sets.
It is dark at **night.**

nine

Nine is a number.
Here are **nine** blocks.

9

no

1. "Do you know the answer?"
   "**No,** I do not know the answer."
2. There is **no** soup for dinner.
   There is not any soup for dinner.

noise

We hear a **noise.**
The fire engine made
a lot of **noise.**

none

Are there any eggs in the nest?
No. There are **none.**
There are not any eggs in the nest.

noon

Noon is the middle of the day.
We eat lunch at **noon.**

north

North is a direction.
It is very cold at the **North** Pole.

nose

I breathe through my **nose.**
I smell with my **nose.**

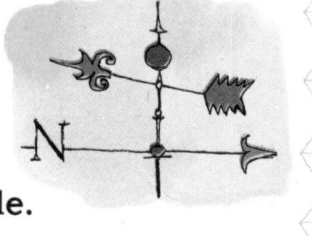

not

Does Bruce go to school?
No. Bruce does **not** go to school.

note

1. Mother wrote a **note.**
   Mother wrote a short letter.
2. I will make a **note** of this.
   I will write it down.
   I will remember about this.

nothing

There is **nothing** on the plate.
There is not anything on the plate.

now

You must go to bed **now.**
You must go to bed this minute.

number   2   36   58

A **number** shows how many or how much.
1. One quart holds two pints.
2. **Number** 4 is a group of four ones.   4   9
3. John had a **number** of books.   75
   He had several books.   1

nurse

A **nurse** looks after sick people.

nut

1. **Nuts** grow on trees.
   They have hard shells.
2. We use metal **nuts** in machines.

O o

The fifteenth letter in the alphabet

oat

Oats are a grain.
Porridge is made from **oats.**
We eat porridge for breakfast.

obey

The dog **obeys** his master.
The dog does as his master tells him.

obeys   obeyed   obeying

ocean

The **ocean** is filled with salt water.
The **ocean** covers most of the earth's surface.
Have you seen the **ocean?**

of

1. He took a piece **of** cake.
   He took some cake.
2. The box is full **of** toffee.
   The box is filled with toffee.
3. He gave a smile **of** joy.
   He smiled with joy.
4. Bill is a boy **of** six years.
   Bill is a boy six **years** old.

off

The leaves are falling **off** the trees.

office

People work in **offices.**
Mother and I go to Father's **office.**

often

We **often** have ice cream.
We have ice cream many times.

oh

We say "**Oh!**" when we are surprised.

oil

Oil is thick liquid.
Oil is found in the ground.
We use **oil** in machines.

old

1. The **old** man can hardly walk.
   When he was young he could run.
2. The **old** shoe is of no use.
   The worn-out shoe is of no use.
3. Jim is six years **old.**
   Jim is six years of age.

on

The flowers are **on** the table.

once

1. **Once** I rode in an aircraft.
   One time I rode in an aircraft.
2. **Once** there was a princess.
   At one time there was a princess.
3. We all eat dinner at **once.**
   We all eat at the same time.
4. Come home at **once!**
   Come home this minute!

one   1

1. **One** is a number.
   Here is **one** lamb.
2. **One** should eat every day.
   A person should eat every day.

onion

Onions are vegetables.
They are good to eat.

only

I have **only** one doll.
I wish I had more dolls.

open

The door is **open.**
Dick **opened** it.

opens   opened   opening

or

Shall we go by bus **or** by train?

orange

1. An **orange** is a round fruit.
2. **Orange** is a colour.

order

1. Everything is in **order.**
   Everything is in its right place.
2. The captain gave the men an **order.**
   The captain said what the men must do.
3. Mother **ordered** the groceries.
   Mother told the grocer what to send.

   orders   ordered   ordering

organ

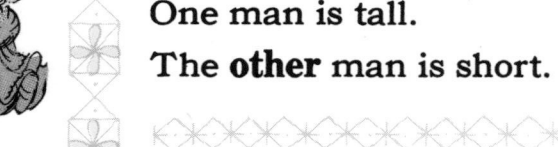

We hear **organ** music
in church.

other

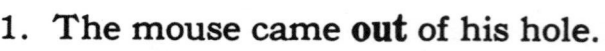

One man is tall.
The **other** man is short.

out

1. The mouse came **out** of his hole.
2. Mother is **out.**
   She is not at home.

58

outside

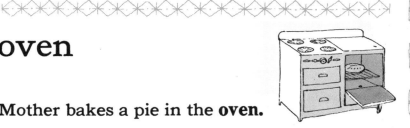

1. The bird is **outside** the nest.
2. We play **outside** in warm weather.
   We play out of doors in warm weather.

oven

Mother bakes a pie in the **oven.**

over

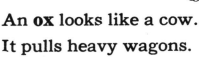

1. The aircraft flew **over** the mountain.
2. You will get **over** your cold.
   Your cold will soon be gone.

owl

An **owl** is a big bird.
Owls hunt at night.

own

I have a rabbit.
He is my very **own.**
He belongs to me.
I **own** him.
I am his **owner.**

owns   owned   owning

ox

An **ox** looks like a cow.
It pulls heavy wagons.

P p

The sixteenth letter in the alphabet

pack

1. Jim **packs** his case.
   He puts his clothes in his case.

2. The man has a **pack** on his back.

packs   packed   packing

package

Ann wrapped up a **package.**

page

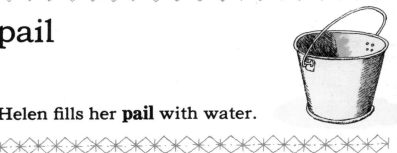

A book has many **pages.**
You are reading a **page** of this book.

pail

Helen fills her **pail** with water.

pain

I have a bad tooth.
It gives me **pain.**
It is **painful.**

59

paint

We colour things with **paint**.
We **paint** pictures with **paints**.
The **painter** is **painting** the door red.

paints   painted   painting

pair

a pair of rabbits   a pair of shoes

Two things which are alike make a **pair**.

palace

A **palace** is the home of a king.

pan

We cook food in **pans**.

pancake

Pancakes are food.
Pancakes are good with butter.

pansy

A **pansy** is a flower.

paper

1. The pages of this book are **paper**.
2. Father sat reading his news**paper**.

papoose

The Red Indian mother calls her baby a **papoose**

parachute

The **parachute** brings the flier safely down.

parade

The circus **parade** goes along the street.

park

1. Mother took Bruce to the **park**.
   Trees and grass grow in the **park**.
2. The car is **parked** in the street.
   The car is left in the street.

parks   parked   parking

part

1. Bill ate **part** of the cake.
   Bill ate some of the cake.
2. Bob **parts** his hair in the middle.

parts   parted   parting

party

The children played games
at the **party**.

pass

1. The train will **pass** the car.
   The train will get ahead of the car.
2. Mother will **pass** round biscuits.
   She will give a biscuit to everyone.

passes   passed   passing

past

1. Everything that has happened
   is in the **past.**
   In the **past** you were a baby.
2. The car went **past** the gate.

paste

Paste is used
for sticking things together.

pat

1. A **pat** of butter is on the plate.

2. John **pats** Rover on the head.
   He **pats** softly with his hand.

pats   patted   patting

patch

Mother sewed a **patch** over the hole.

path

The **path** leads to the gate.

pay

Jim's father **pays**
for his newspaper.

pays   paid   paying

pea

A **pea** is a vegetable.
It is a green seed of a plant.
Peas are good to eat.

peach

A **peach** is a fruit.
It has a fuzzy skin.

peanut

Peanuts are good to eat.

pear

A **pear** is a fruit.
Pears grow on trees.

pen

1. We write with a **pen** and ink.

2. Sheep are sometimes
   put in a **pen.**

pencil

We use a **pencil** for writing.

pending

The results of my exams are **pending.**
I am waiting to hear my exam results.

people

Men and women are **people.**
Boys and girls are **people.**

perhaps

Perhaps the cloud will bring rain.
It may rain. It may not rain.

person

A **person** is a man or woman, boy or girl.

pet

Pets are animals we keep as friends.
Dan feeds his **pet** rabbit.

piano

We hear music when Mother
plays the **piano.**

pick

1. The man works with a **pick.**
2. Beth **picks** flowers.
3. You may **pick** a doll.
   You may choose a doll.

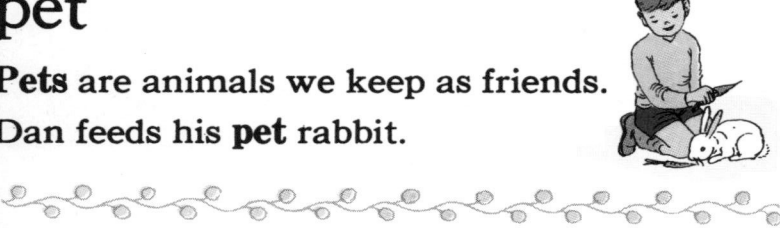

picks   picked   picking

picnic

Our family went on a **picnic.**

picture

The **pictures** in this book are coloured.

pie

We often have **pie** for dinner.

piece

I cut a **piece** of the pie.

pig

A **pig** is an animal.

pigeon

A **pigeon** is a bird.
The message was sent by carrier **pigeon.**

pillow

I sleep with my head
on a **pillow.**

pin

We fasten things together
with **pins.**
Ruth **pinned** a flower on her dress

pins   pinned   pinning

pineapple

A **pineapple** is a big fruit.

pink

Pink is a colour.

pint

A **pint** is a measure
for liquids.
A small milk bottle holds a half **pint**.

pipe

1. Water comes to our house through **pipes.**
2. Father smokes a **pipe.**

place

1. There is a **place** for Bruce
   at the table.
2. Where did you **place** the chair?
   Where did you put the chair?

places   placed   placing

plain

1. I have a **plain** sheet of paper.
   There is nothing on it.
2. Is it **plain** to you?
   Can you understand it?

plan

Mother will **plan** the party.
Before the party she will think
of what we need.

plans   planned   planning

plant

1. A **plant** is a living thing
   that does not move about.
   This **plant** grows in a pot.

2. A **plant** is a factory.
   Workmen make things in **plants.**

3. We **plant** seeds in the earth.

plants   planted   planting

plate

I eat from a blue **plate.**

play

1. We acted in a **play** at school.
2. We **play** after school.
   We have fun after school.
   My **play** mate and I **play** with
   our **play** things.

plays   played   playing

please

1. "Will you **please** give me a biscuit?"
2. The toy will **please** the baby.
   It will make him happy.

pleases   pleased   pleasing

plenty

We have **plenty** of time to catch the bus.
We have all the time we need to catch the bus.

plough

A **plough** is used
for turning over the soil.
The farmer **ploughs** the field.

plough   ploughed   ploughing

plum

A **plum** is a juicy fruit.
Plums are good to eat.

pocket

Bill has a handkerchief in his **pocket.**

point

1. The **point** of the pencil is the sharp end.

2. The church spire **points**
   to the sky.
   The teacher is **pointing** at
   the blackboard with the **pointer.**

points   pointed   pointing

pole

The **pole** holds up the clothes-line.

policeman

A **policeman** keeps order among people.
He helps us to cross the street.

polite

A **polite** person is pleasant and good
to other people.

pony

A **pony** is a small horse.

poor

1. **Poor** people have not much money.
2. Betty's work is **poor.**
   It is not good work.

possible

1. Is it **possible** to fly to the moon?
   Can people fly to the moon?
2. Is it **possible** that George is sick?
   Is he really sick?

64

post

1. The **post** stands in the ground.

2. The **post** office stamps our letters.
   The **post**man delivers our letters.

pot

We keep many different things in **pots.**

potato

A **potato** is a vegetable.
Potatoes grow in the ground.

pound

1. A **pound** is a measure of weight.
   How many **pounds** do you weigh?
2. A **pound** is money.
   There are one hundred pence in a **pound.**
3. Bill is **pounding** nails.
   He is hammering nails.

   pounds   pounded   pounding

pour

Lucy **pours** the milk
from the jug into the glass.

   pours   poured   pouring

pray

Ellen is saying her **prayers.**
When we **pray** we talk to God.

   prays   prayed   praying

present

1. The **present** is now.
   Yesterday is the past.
2. There are **presents** under the tree.
   There are gifts under the tree.

press

1. Ruth will **press** the switch
   to turn on the light.
2. Mother **presses** the clothes
   with an iron.

   presses   pressed   pressing

pretty

Mary had a **pretty** ribbon in her hair.
The ribbon was nice to look at.

price

What is the **price** of the book?
How much money do I have to pay for it?

prince

A **prince** is the son of
a king and a queen.

princess

A **princess** is the daughter
of a king and a queen.

print

1. Rover left foot**prints.**

2. Can you **print** your name?

3. This book was **printed** on a **printing** press.

   prints   printed   printing

pudding

Pudding is a sweet.

It is sweet.

pull

Tom **pulls** his cart.

pulls   pulled   pulling

puppy

A **puppy** is a young dog.

purple

Purple is a colour.

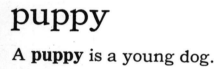

Q q

The seventeenth letter of the alphabet

quart

A **quart** is a measure of liquids.

There are two pints in a **quart.**

purse

Mother keeps her money in a **purse.**

push

Ann **pushes** the pram.

pushes   pushed   pushing

put

Tom **puts** his hat on his head.

puts   put   putting

puzzle

Ann and Bob have a **puzzle.**

They are putting the pieces together

to make a picture.

pyjamas

Peter is wearing **pyjamas.**

He is ready for bed.

quarter

1. This pie is divided into four **quarters.**

   This pie is divided into four equal parts.

2. We eat supper at

   quarter past seven.

queen

A **queen** is the wife of a king.

Sometimes she reigns alone.

66

question

We ask a **question** when we want to know something.
"Is it raining?" is a **question.**

quick

To be **quick** is to do something fast.
Tom ran **quickly.**

quiet

To be **quiet** is to make no noise.
Jack is **quiet** because he is asleep.

quite

1. The glass is **quite** full.
   The glass is just full.
2. The rose is **quite** red.
   The rose is very red.

R r

The eighteenth letter of the alphabet

rabbit

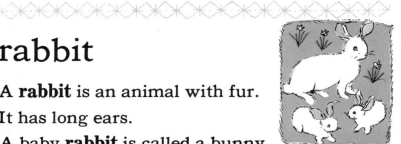

A **rabbit** is an animal with fur.
It has long ears.
A baby **rabbit** is called a bunny.

race

The boys had a **race** to see who could run fastest.

radio

We hear voices and music over the **radio.**

rail

1. The train runs on **rails.**
2. There is a **rail** around the verandah.

rain

The **rain** comes down in drops of water.

rainbow

See the **rainbow** in the sky!

rat

A **rat** is a small animal.
It has a long tail.

rather

Which would you **rather** have?
Which would you like to have most?

reach

Bruce tries to **reach** the bin.
reaches   reached   reaching

67

read

We **read** stories in books.

reads   read   reading

ready

Are you **ready** for school?

Have you all your things to take to school?

real

This is only a picture of a brush.

I brush my hair with a **real** brush.

reason

Why did you close the window?

What was your **reason** for closing it?

red

Red is a colour.

When the traffic light is **red,** it means STOP.

refrigerator

A **refrigerator** keeps food cold.

reindeer

A **reindeer** is an animal
which lives in the cold north.

Reindeer pull Santa Claus's sleigh.

remember

Did you **remember** to bring your book?

Did you think to bring it?

remembers   remembered   remembering

reply

1. Father wrote me a letter.

   I will write a **reply** to it.

   I will write a letter back to him.

2. "Is it raining?" asked Mother.

   "Yes, Mother," **replied** John.

   replies   replied   replying

rest

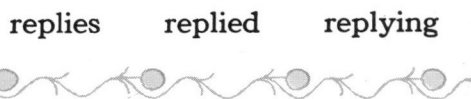

1. The tired dog takes a **rest.**

2. One apple is on the table.

   The **rest** of the apples are in the basket.

return

Father went away last week.

He will **return** tomorrow.

He will come back tomorrow.

returns   returned   returning

ribbon

We use pretty **ribbon** for tying things.

rice

Rice is a cereal.

It grows in wet earth.

rich

1. The **rich** man has a lot of money.
2. The pie is **rich.**
   It is very sweet.

ride

We **ride** in the bus.
Tom **rides** his bicycle.

rides   rode   ridden   riding

right

1. I have a **right** hand
   and a left hand.

2. Is it **right** to cross the road anywhere?
   No. It is wrong.
   It is **right** to cross
   at the crossing.

3. The ball fell **right** into the basket.

ring

1. Mother's **ring** has a jewel in it.
2. The bells **ring** on Christmas day.

    rings   rang   rung   ringing

ripe

When fruit is **ripe,** we can eat it.
When it is not **ripe,** it does not taste good.

rise

To **rise** is to get up or to go up.
The balloon **rises** in the air.

    rises   rose   risen   rising

river

The **river** flows down to the sea.

road

The cars go along the **road.**

roar

Did you ever hear a lion **roar?**
Roaring is a loud noise.

    roars   roared   roaring

robin

A **robin** is a bird with a red breast.

rock

1. A **rock** is a big stone.
   There are **rocks**
   along the ocean shore.
2. Jean **rocks** the baby to sleep.

    rocks   rocked   rocking

roll

1. We **roll** down the hill.

2. The paper is in a **roll.**

3. Jim wears **roller** skates.

4. I had a **roll** for breakfast.

    rolls   rolled   rolling

roof

The house has a red **roof.**

room

1. The **room** is full of furniture.
2. Is there **room** for Harry in the wagon?

root

The **roots** of plants grow in the earth.

rope

The **rope** is long and strong.
Peter jumps with a **rope.**

rose

A **rose** is a flower.
A **rose** has a sweet smell.

rough

1. The dog has a **rough** coat.
   The ocean is **rough** during a storm.

2. In a **rough** game the boys may get hurt.

round

1. The ball is **round.**
2. The train goes **round** the tracks.

row

1. The lilies grow in a **row.**
   They are growing side by side.

rub

Bill **rubs** the chalk off the board.
    rubs   rubbed   rubbing

rubber

1. We use a piece of **rubber**
   to rub out pencil marks.
   We call it an eraser.
2. We wear **rubber** boots in the rain.
   These things are made from **rubber.**

rug

We have a blue **rug** on our floor.

rule

1. It is a **rule** in our house to get up early.
   Everyone in our house must get up early.
2. We use a foot **rule** to measure length.

run

1. Tom can **run** fast.
2. A railway line **runs** through our city.
   It goes through our city.

   runs   ran   running

rush

To **rush** means to do something quickly.
The fire engine **rushes** to the fire.

rushes   rushed   rushing

S s

The nineteenth letter of the alphabet

sack

A **sack** is a large bag.
The **sack** is full of potatoes.

sad

Mary is **sad**
because she broke her doll.
She is unhappy.

safe

It is not **safe** to play in the street.
If you keep the **safety** rules,
you will not be hurt.

sail

A **sail** is made of cloth.
The wind presses against the **sail**
and makes the **sailing**-boat move.
We like to go **sailing.**

sails   sailed   sailing

sailor

A **sailor** works on a ship.

salt

Salt is dug from the earth.
We put **salt** on our food.
It makes food taste better.

same

My birthday is on May 1st.
Julie's birthday is on May 1st.
Our birthdays are on the **same** day.

sand

The beach is full of **sand.**
The children play in the **sand.**

sandwich

I made a **sandwich**
with bread and ham.

Santa Claus

Santa Claus comes down
the chimney on Christmas Eve.
He fills our stockings with toys.

save

1. Do you **save** your money?
   Do you keep your money?

2. The man swam to **save** the boy.
   The man went to help the boy.

saves   saved   saving

saw

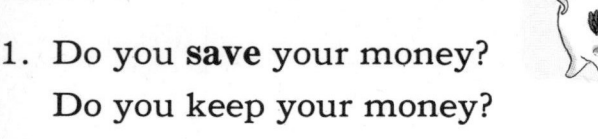

A **saw** is used for cutting wood.
It has an edge with sharp teeth.

scale

1. A **scale** is used to weigh things.
   A pound of sugar is on the **scale.**

2. Some fish are covered with **scales.**

school

We go to **school** to learn.

scissors

Scissors are used for cutting.

scratch

The cat made a **scratch** on the chair.
We can **scratch** with our fingernails.

scratches   scratched   scratching

screw

This is a **screw.**
Screws hold things together.

scrub

Annie **scrubs** the floor
with soap and water.

scrubs   scrubbed   scrubbing

sea

The **sea** is full of salt water.
It is also called the ocean.
Ships sail on the **sea.**

season

There are four **seasons** in the year.
They are spring, summer, autumn, and winter.

seat

A **seat** is something to sit on.

see

We **see** with our eyes.
When our eyes are closed we cannot **see.**

sees   saw   seen   seeing

seed

Plants grow from **seeds.**
You will find **seeds**
in many fruits and vegetables.

seem

What the dog saw in the mirror
seemed to be another dog.

seems   seemed   seeming

sell

The grocer **sells** groceries.

He gives us groceries for money.

sells   sold   selling

send

1. I will **send** a letter.

   I will put a letter in the pillar-box.

2. Mother **sent** me to the shop.

   Mother told me to go to the shop,

   and I went.

   sends   sent   sending

set

1. The things are **set** on the table.

   They are put on the table.

2. The sun is **setting.**

   The sun is going down.

   sets   set   setting

seven 7

Seven is a number.

Here are **seven** ducks.

sew

We **sew** cloth.

Mother is **sewing** a dress.

She uses a needle and thread.

sews   sewed   sewing

shade

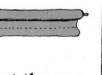

A window **shade** keeps out the sun.

It is cooler in the **shade** than in the sun.

shadow

Betty's **shadow** is on the wall.

shake

Mother **shakes** the dust out
of the rug.

We **shake** hands when we meet
our friends.

shakes   shook   shaking

shall

1. I **shall** go tomorrow.

   I am going tomorrow.

2. He **shall** give you back the doll.

   He has to give it back.

   should

shape

These boxes have different **shapes.**

share

1. We **share** the biscuits.

   We divide them among us.

2. I gave my **share** to Bruce.

   I gave my part to Bruce.

   shares   shared   sharing

sharp

The pencil point is **sharp.**

The knife is **sharp.**

We cut with the **sharp** edge of the knife.

73

she

This is Ann.
She is a girl.
Her coat is red.
She plays by **herself** with her doll.

her   hers   herself

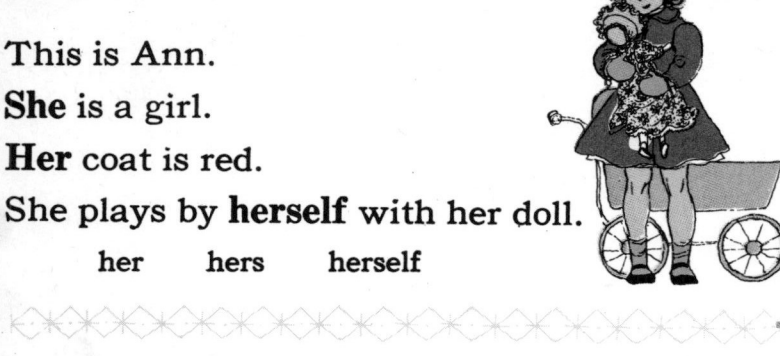

sheep

A **sheep** is an animal.
We get wool from **sheep.**

shelf

The **shelf** is painted green.

shell

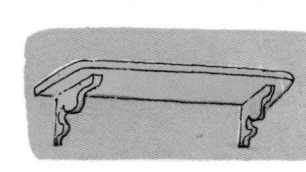

1. Some sea animals are covered with **shells.**
   We find sea**shells** on the beach.
2. An egg has a **shell.**

shine

1. The moon **shines** on the water.

2. Pete **shines** his shoes.

shines   shined   shone   shining

ship

Ships sail on the sea.

shirt

Men and boys wear **shirts.**

shoe

We wear **shoes** on our feet.

shoot

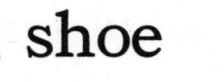

Bill **shoots** his gun.

shoots   shot   shooting

shop

Mother goes **shopping** for food.
She goes to the butcher **shop** to buy meat.

shops   shopped   shopping

shore

The **shore** is by the edge of the sea.
Rivers and lakes have **shores.**
We play in the sand on the **shore.**

short

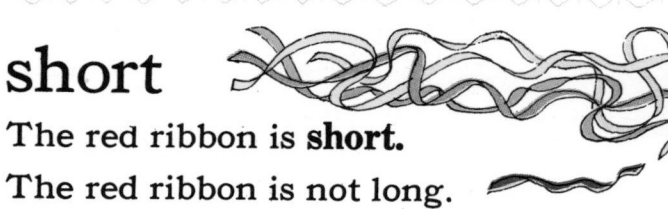

The red ribbon is **short.**
The red ribbon is not long.

shoulder

The bird perched
on the man's **shoulder.**

shovel

Ed cleaned the path
with a snow **shovel.**
A steam **shovel** digs big holes.

74

show

1. I will **show** you my rabbit.
   I will let you see my rabbit.
2. The children in our street
   had a pet **show.**

   shows   showed   showing

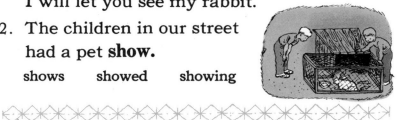

sick

Tom is **sick.**

He is not feeling well.

side

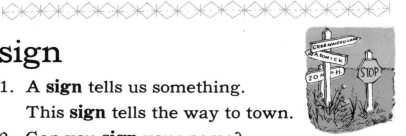

1. My right arm is on my right **side.**
   My left arm is on my left **side.**

2. A tree grows at the **side** of the house.

sign

1. A **sign** tells us something.
   This **sign** tells the way to town.
2. Can you **sign** your name?
   Can you write your name?

   John Smith

   signs   signed   signing

silent

The house was **silent.**

There was no sound in the house.

silk

Silk thread is made by **silk**worms.

We make **silk** into cloth.

silver

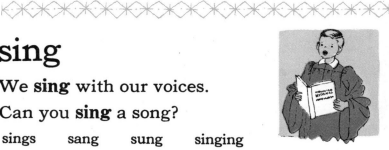

Silver is a metal.

Mother has spoons, forks,

and other things made of **silver.**

sing

We **sing** with our voices.

Can you **sing** a song?

sings   sang   sung   singing

sink

1. The water runs down the **sink.**

2. The brick **sinks** in the water.
   It goes to the bottom.

   sinks   sank   sunk   sinking

sister

Betty is my **sister.**

We have the same mother and father

sit

I **sit** in a chair.

sits   sat   sitting

six

6

Six is a number.

Here are **six** bunnies.

size

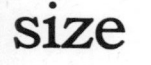

1. What **size** is your coat?
   How big is your coat?
2. The brown dog is of a larger
   size than the white dog.

skate

1. We will **skate** on the ice.
2. We wear **skates** on our feet.
   skates   skated   skating

skin

1. Our bodies are covered with **skin.**
2. An orange has a thick **skin.**

skip

Lily **skips** with a rope.
skips   skipped   skipping

sky

We see the sun, moon, stars,
and clouds in the **sky.**

sledge

We like to slide on a **sledge.**

sleep

We go to **sleep** at night.
sleeps   slept   sleeping

sleigh

We ride over the snow
in a **sleigh.**

slide

1. Tom and Ann **slide** on the ice.
2. I **slide** down the **slide.**
   slides   slid   sliding

slip

1. Write your name on a **slip** of paper.
2. Bill's foot **slipped.**
   slips   slipped   slipping

slow

The tortoise is **slow.**
The tortoise goes **slowly.**

small

A pea is **small.**
It is very little.

smell

1. The rose has a sweet **smell.**
2. We **smell** with our noses.
   smells   smelled   smelling

smile

We **smile** when we are happy.
Bob is **smiling.**
smiles   smiled   smiling

smoke

1. Grey **smoke** goes up from the fire.
2. Father is **smoking** a pipe.

smokes   smoked   smoking

smooth

Silk is **smooth** to touch.

snail

The **snail** has a shell on his back.

snake

The **snake** is an animal with no legs.
The **snake** crawls along.

sneeze

"Atchoo!"
Tom's cold made him **sneeze.**

sneezes   sneezed   sneezing

snow

Snow comes in winter.
It falls in white flakes.

so

1. Rover ran **so** fast he got tired.
2. I am not **so** sure as you are.
   I am not as sure as you are.
3. Do you think it is **so?**
   Do you believe it is true?
4. I will go and **so** will you.
   I will go and you will, too.

soap

We wash things clean with **soap.**

sock

We wear **socks** on our feet.

soft

The pillow is **soft.**

soldier

The **soldier** is in the army.

some

1. **Some** of the apples are green.
   A number of the apples are green.
2. **Some** ink fell on the cloth.
   Drops of ink fell on the cloth.

something

Something is in the box.
What is it?

sometimes

Sometimes there is a rainbow.
There are times when there is a rainbow.

son

Bill is the **son** of his father
and his mother.

song

We sing a **song.**

soon

Soon it will be dinner time.
In a short time
it will be dinner time.

sort

Harry **sorts** his marbles.
He puts the green ones together
and the brown ones together.

sorts   sorted   sorting

sound

I hear the **sound** of voices.
I hear the noise of voices.

soup

Soup is a liquid food.
I had a bowl of tomato **soup.**

south

South is a direction.
South is opposite to north.
The birds fly **south** in the winter.

spade

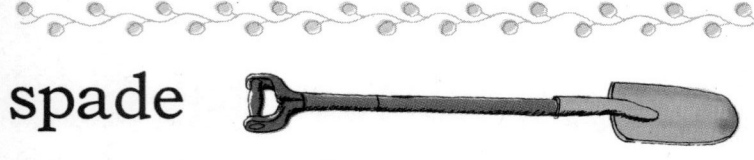

We dig with a **spade.**

speak

Peter **speaks** to the class.
He tells them about his trip.

speaks   spoke   spoken   speaking

spill

Mary **spills** a glass of water.

spills   spilled   spilling

spoon

We eat with a **spoon.**

spot

The leopard has **spots** on his coat.

The ink made a **spot** on the cloth.

spring

1. The flowers bloom
   in the **spring** of the year.

2. The **spring** came out of the watch.

square

A draughts board is **square.**

stairs

The **stairs** are painted red.

stamp

1. The letter has a **stamp** in the corner.
2. The horse **stamped** his hoof.

stamps stamped stamping

stand

1. We bought melons at the fruit **stand.**
2. I **stand** on two legs.

stands stood standing

star

The **stars** shine at night.

state

There are 50 **states**
in the United States of America.

station

Trains stop at the railway **station.**

step

1. The baby took his first **step.**
2. The ladder has six **steps.**

stick

A **stick** is a small piece of wood.

still

1. The water is **still.**
   It does not move.
2. Rover is **still.**
   He is quiet.
3. Are you **still** in bed?
   Are you not out of bed yet?

stocking

We wear **stockings** on our legs.

stone

A **stone** is small and very hard.
The farmer made a **stone** wall.
Jewels are beautiful **stones.**

stop

The car comes to a **stop**
at the red light.
It does not move.

store

1. We buy things in a **store.**
2. The squirrel **stores** nuts.
   The squirrel saves nuts.

stores stored storing

storm

A **storm** is bad weather.
It rains and blows and sometimes snows.

79

story

I like the **story** of Cinderella.

stove

We use **stoves** for cooking.

straight

The ruler is **straight.**

stream

A **stream** is a little river.

street

There are houses
on both sides of the **street.**

string

We use **string** for tying things.

strong

1. The **strong** man lifts the weights.
2. Iron is **strong.**
   It does not break easily.

such

I have never had **such** good biscuits.
I have never had biscuits as good as these.

sudden

All of a **sudden** the sun came out.
All at once the sun came out.
Suddenly the sun came out.

sugar

Sugar is sweet.
Sugar is made from **sugar** cane.

suit

A **suit** is clothing.
A **suit** has matching jacket
and trousers or skirt.

summer

Summer is the warmest
season of the year.

sun

The **sun** is setting.
We like to swim on warm, **sunny** days.
We like to play in the **sun**shine.

supper

Supper is the last meal of the day.

suppose

Do you **suppose** Santa Claus will come?
Do you think he will come?

supposes   supposed   supposing

80

sure

"Has the rain stopped?"
"I will look to make **sure.**"

surprise

1. Mother had a **surprise** for Jim.
   He did not know she had made biscuits.
2. Ruth was **surprised** to see her father.
   He **surprised** her by coming home early.

   surprises   surprised   surprising

sweet

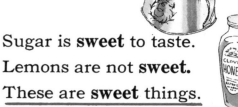

Sugar is **sweet** to taste.
Lemons are not **sweet.**
These are **sweet** things.

swim

Tom **swims** in the water.

swims   swam   swum   swimming

sweep

Bill **sweeps** up the dust.

sweeps   swept   sweeping

swing

Lucy **swings** in her **swing.**

swings   swung   swinging

T t

The twentieth letter in the alphabet

talk

Our baby is learning to **talk.**
He has learned to say some words.

talks   talked   talking

table

A **table** is a piece of furniture.
It has four legs and a flat top.

tall

The building is **tall.**
The building is very high.

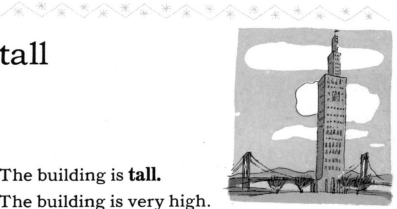

tail

Some animals have **tails.**
A squirrel has a long bushy **tail.**

taste

We **taste** with our tongues.
Lollipops **taste** good.

tastes   tasted   tasting

take

Sue **takes** her books to school.

takes   took   taken   taking

81

teach

Mother **teaches** Ann to cook.
She tells her how to cook.
Our **teacher teaches** us
our lessons.

teaches   taught   teaching

telephone

We talk to people over the **telephone.**

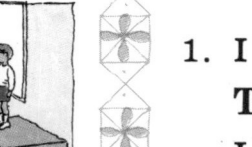

tell

Tell a story to the class.

tells   told   telling

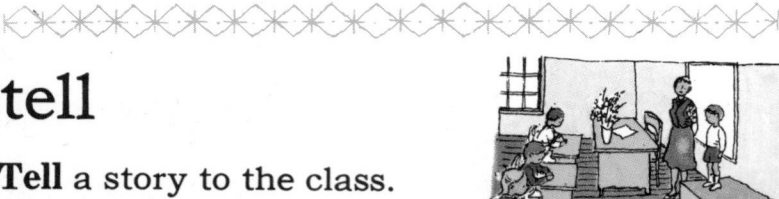

ten   10

Ten is a number.
Here are **ten** ducks.

tent

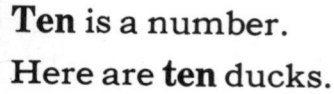

The boys put up a **tent.**

than

I am taller **than** you.
You are not so tall as I am.

thank

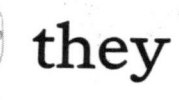

We **thank** people when they are kind.
"**Thank** you for the sweet," says John.

thanks   thanked   thanking

that

That bird in the sky is a crow.
Those birds on the ground are chickens.

the

A petal fell off **the** rose.

then

1. I will read the book.
   Then I will take it back.
   I will take it back
   after I have read it.
2. Mother was a little girl **then.**
   Mother was a little girl at that time.

there

We will go **there** by train.
We will go to that place by train.

they

My friends are here.
They have come to play.

thick

1. The book is **thick.**
   It has many pages.
2. Hansel and Gretel walked
   through the **thick** forest.
   The trees in the forest grow
   close together.

82

thin

1. The tall man is **thin**.
   He is not fat.
2. The clown's hair is **thin**.
   There is not much of it.

thing

A house is a **thing** you can see.
A song is a **thing** you can hear.
Smoke is a **thing** you can smell.

think

We **think** with our minds.
Bob is **thinking** about his homework.

thinks   thought   thinking

this

This is a squirrel in the tree.
These are bears on the ground.

thread

Mother uses **thread** for sewing.

three

3

Three is a number.
Here are **three** dogs.

through

1. Tom went **through** the doorway.
2. Bob is **through** with his homework.
   He has finished it.

throw

Peter **throws** the ball.

throws   threw   thrown   throwing

thumb

The **thumb** is shorter than the fingers.

ticket

Pat got a **ticket** when he paid to see the circus.

tie

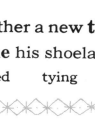

1. We gave Father a new **tie**.
2. Bruce can **tie** his shoelaces.

ties   tied   tying

time

1. The clock tells us what **time** it is.
2. What **time** does the train leave?
   When does it leave?
3. Mother has no **time** to help me.
   Mother has other things to do.

to

1. Bill walks from the gate **to** the door.
2. Bob is kind **to** his dog.
3. Are you going **to** walk?

83

tool

saw, hammer, trowel, shears, plane, drill, knife, level, wrench, soldering iron, screwdriver, chisel, pick, axe, square, spade, shovel, hoe, rake, fork, trowel

We use **tools** to work with.

These are tools.

tooth

Our baby has one **tooth.**

We use our **teeth** for biting food.

top

1. Robert is sitting on the **top** of the stepladder.

2. Dick has a red-and-yellow **top.**

touch

Touch the ice and see how cold it is.

Put your hand on the ice.

touches   touched   touching

towel

We use a **towel** to dry ourselves.

today

Today is my birthday.

This day is my birthday.

toe

A **toe** is part of the foot.

I have five **toes** on each foot.

My shoes have square **toes.**

together

Betty and Ann play **together.**

They play with each other.

tomato

A **tomato** is good to eat.

We grow **tomatoes** in our garden.

tomorrow

Tomorrow is the day after today.

tongue

Peter put his **tongue** out.

Our **tongues** help us to speak.

too

1. May Rover come **too?**

   May Rover come also?

2. Mary's soup is **too** hot.

   It is so hot that she cannot sip it.

town

A **town** is smaller than a city.

toy

We play with our **toys.**
These are **toys.**

tree

fir tree

These are **trees.**   oak tree   apple tree   palm tree

There are many kinds of **trees.**

trip

1. We took a **trip** in the country.

   We went travelling in the country.

2. Jim will **trip** on that rug.

   He will stumble on the rug.

   trips   tripped   tripping

true

1. Water is wet.

   This is **true.**

2. Mother read us a fairy tale.

   The fairy tale was not **true.**

trumpet

John plays the **trumpet.**
John makes music with the **trumpet.**

try

Try to thread the needle.
See if you can do it.
tries   tried   trying

tub

wash-tub

We often put water in **tubs.**   bath tub

turn

1. The car **turned** the corner.

2. **My turn** is after your **turn.**

   I do it after you do it.

   turns   turned   turning

twin

Tom and Tim are **twins.**
They look alike.

two

Two is a number.
Here are **two** elephants.

typewriter

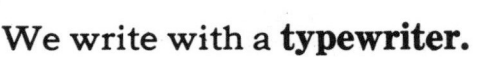

We write with a **typewriter**.

U u

The twenty-first letter in the alphabet

until

We must stay in **until** the rain stops.
We must not go out before then.

umbrella

An **umbrella** keeps off the rain.

up

The aircraft is going **up**.

under

1. The boat goes **under** the bridge.
2. Four is a number **under** five.

upon

Bill puts one block **upon** another.

understand

Do you **understand** your lessons?
Do you know how to do them?

understands   understood   understanding

use

A knife has a **use**.
It is **used** for cutting.
It is **useful** for cutting.

uses   used   using

V v

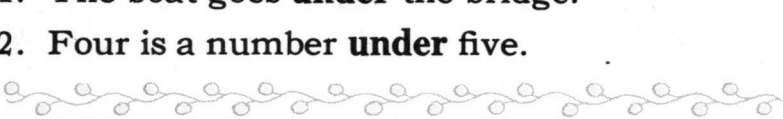

The twenty-second letter in the alphabet

vase

Mary puts some flowers in a **vase**.

Valentine

Valentine's Day is February 14th.
This is a **valentine**.

vegetable

We grow **vegetables** for food.
These are **vegetables.**

vehicle

Some **vehicles** carry people.
Some **vehicles** carry things.
<u>These are **vehicles.**</u>

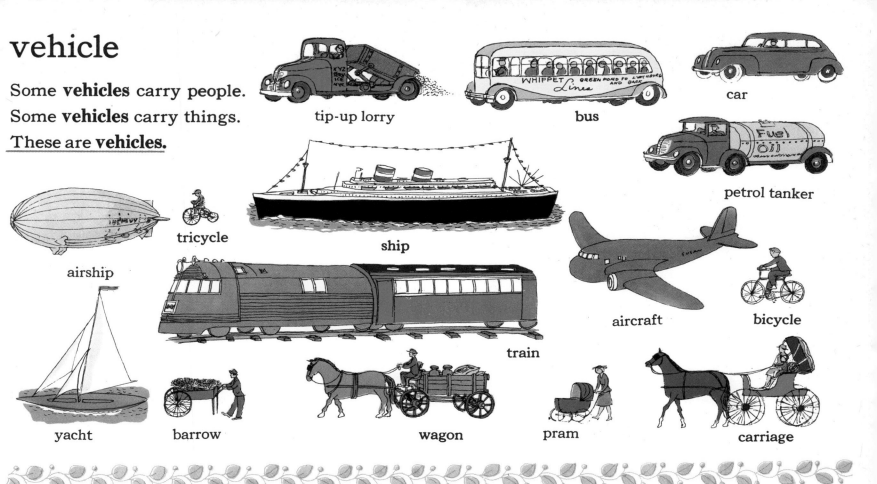

tip-up lorry

bus

car

petrol tanker

ship

airship

tricycle

aircraft

bicycle

train

yacht

barrow

wagon

pram

carriage

very

The mouse is **very** small.

view

We have a **view** from the window.
We can see outdoors.

village

There are only a few houses
in a **village.**

vine

A **vine** is a climbing plant.

violet

A **violet** is a wild flower.
Violet is a colour.

violin

A **violin** makes sweet music.

visit

Ann went to **visit** Betty.
She went to see Betty,
at Betty's house.
She was Betty's **visitor.**

visits   visited   visiting

voice

I speak with my **voice.**
I sing with my **voice.**

87

W w

The twenty-third letter in the alphabet

wagon

The toy **wagon** is red.
The **wagon** is full of hay.

waist

Sue has a red belt round her **waist.**

wait

Bill is **waiting** for the postman.
The postman will come soon.

waits   waited   waiting

walk
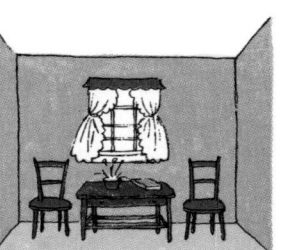

We **walk** on our legs.
Peter is **walking** to school.

walks   walked   walking

wall

Our house has four **walls.**
There is a window
in one **wall** of my room.

want

Do you **want** a book?
Would you like to have a book?

wants   wanted   wanting

war

When countries are at **war**
they are fighting each other.

warm
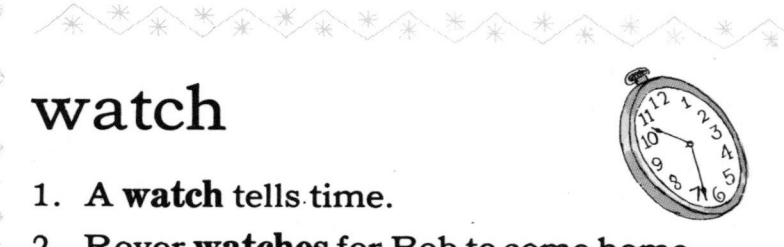

The fire makes us **warm.**
If we get too near, it makes us hot.
Bob **warms** his hands by the fire.

warms   warmed   warming

waste

We **waste** things when we do not use them well.
Waste paper goes in the **waste**paper basket.

wastes   wasted   wasting

watch

1. A **watch** tells time.
2. Rover **watches** for Bob to come home.
   He sits waiting for Bob.

watches   watched   watching

water

Water is a liquid.
It has no colour, smell, or taste.
Water is good to drink.

wave

1. There are **waves** on the sea.
2. Ruth has **waves** in her hair.
3. Mother **waves** good-bye.
4. The flag is **waving** in the wind.

waves   waved   waving

way

1. It is a long **way** home.
   It is a long distance home.
2. This is the **way** to sew.
   This is how you sew.

we

We are two children.
Our names are Ann and Jim.
We go to school by **ourselves.**

us   our   ourselves   ours

wear

1. Betty has a new dress to **wear.**
2. John will **wear** out his trousers.
   I **wore** out mine by sliding.

wears   wore   worn   wearing

weather

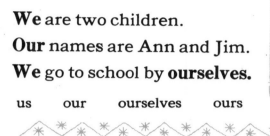

Sunshine makes clear **weather.**
Rain makes wet **weather.**
Fog is bad **weather** for ships.

week

There are seven days in a **week.**
A **week** is a measure of time.

weigh

Jane **weighs** 4 stones.
Her **weight** is 4 stones.

weighs   weighed   weighing

well

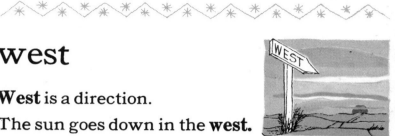

1. John says he is quite **well.**
   He says he is not sick.
2. He did his work **well.**
   He did good work.
3. We drew water from the **well.**

west

West is a direction.
The sun goes down in the **west.**

wet

The **wet** dog has been in the water.

what

What is in the box?

wheat

Wheat is a cereal.
We make bread from **wheat.**

wheel

Wheels are round.
Cars and trains run on **wheels.**
Wheels are parts of machines.

when

When will the clock strike six?
In five minutes.

where

Where is my hat?

It is on your head!

which

Which is the chocolate cake?

The brown one is chocolate.

while

We whistle **while** we work.

whisper

Sue **whispers** in Mother's ear.

She speaks in a low soft voice.

whispers   whispered   whispering

whistle

Bob **whistles** as he walks along.

He blows a tune through his lips.

whistles   whistled   whistling

white

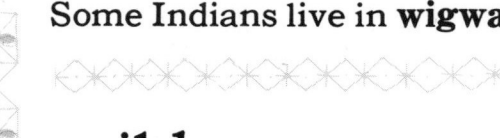

White is a colour.

Snow is **white**.

who

Who is at the door?

Is it Father?

Is it the postman?

whole

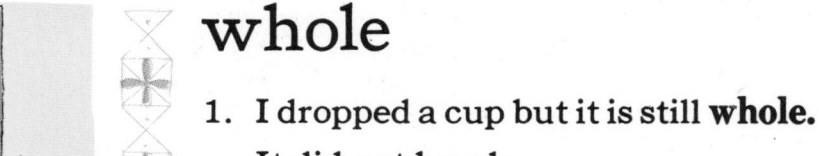

1. I dropped a cup but it is still **whole.**
   It did not break.
2. George ate the **whole** apple.
   He ate all of it.

why

Why do you want your dinner?

Because I am hungry.

wide

The brook is **wide.**

I cannot jump across it.

wigwam

Some Indians live in **wigwams.**

wild

Wild flowers grow in the woods
and fields.

Wild animals do not live near people.

They keep away from people.

will

Will you please post my letter?

Yes, I **will.**

wind

The **wind** blows in the trees.

It is a **windy** day.

90

wind

Bob **winds** the string around his finger.
I **wound** it around my finger, too.

    winds   wound   winding

window

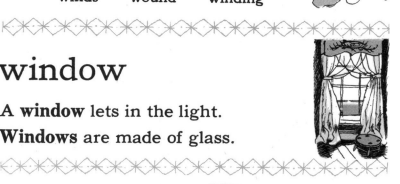

A **window** lets in the light.
Windows are made of glass.

wing

The bird flies on two **wings**.
The aircraft has red **wings**.

winter

Winter is the coldest season of the year.

wipe

Ann **wipes** her hands.
She gets them dry with a towel.

    wipes   wiped   wiping

wire

Wire is made of metal.

wish

1. You may make a **wish.**
   You may think of something you want.
2. I **wish** I were a fireman.
   I would like to be a fireman.

    wishes   wished   wishing

witch

A **witch** flies on a broom.

with

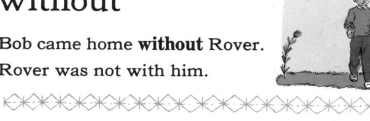

Rover went **with** Bob.
Rover and Bob went together.

without

Bob came home **without** Rover.
Rover was not with him.

wolf

A **wolf** is a wild animal.

woman

My mother is a **woman.**
These are women.

wood

We get **wood** from trees.

1. The **wood** is cut from trees.

2. Trees grow in the **woods.**

wool

A sheep has a coat of **wool.**
We make clothes from **wool.**

91

word

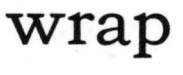

man   fun
good   jump
doll   cat
    Mary

Every **word** tells something.
These are **words.**

work

Everyone has **work** to do.
I **work** at my lessons.
Father **works** in the city.
Mother **works** in our home.

works   worked   working

world

Our **world** is round.
It is called the Earth.

X x

The twenty-fourth letter in the alphabet.

Xmas

Xmas is a short way
of writing Christmas.

Y y

The twenty-fifth letter in the alphabet

wrap

Sue **wraps** her book.
She puts paper around it.

wraps   wrapped   wrapping

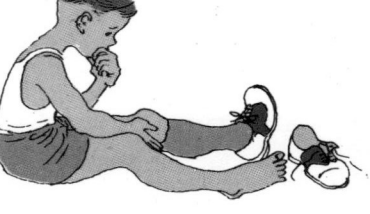

write

Peter **writes** on the board.

writes   wrote   written   writing

wrong

1. Sam has his shoe on the **wrong** foot.
   It should be on the other foot.
2. The dog chewed Father's shoe.
   The dog was **wrong**.

X-ray

An **X-ray** enables us to
see through solid things.

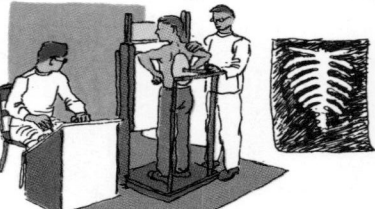

xylophone

I play music on the **xylophone**
with little hammers.

yard

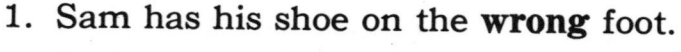

1. A **yard** is a measure.
   It is 3 feet long.
2. There are chickens in the **yard.**

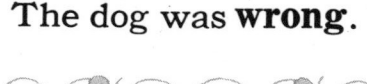
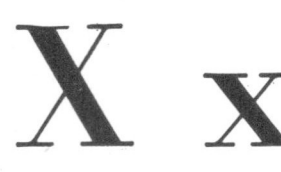

92

yarn

Mother knits with **yarn.**
Yarn is made of wool.

yawn

We **yawn** when we get sleepy.

yawns   yawned   yawning

year

There are twelve months in a **year.**
How many **years** old are you?

yellow

Yellow is a colour.

yes

Is it raining?
Yes, it is raining.

Z z

The twenty-sixth letter in the alphabet

zebra

A **zebra** is a striped animal.
It is something like a horse.

zero

Zero is a number.
Zero means none at all.

yesterday

Yesterday is the day before today.

yet

Have the eggs hatched **yet?**
No, they will hatch tomorrow.

yolk

The **yolk** is the yellow part of the egg.

you

You are reading this book.
What is **your** name?

young

Bruce is **young.**
He is only two years old.

zig-zag

The red line is **zig-zag.**
The red line goes back and forth.

zoo

Father took us to the **zoo.**
We saw many animals.

A NOTE TO PARENTS AND TEACHERS

The *Golden Dictionary* is a book for parents and teachers to share and enjoy with children. It will be of great value to children in building an easy familiarity with words and their uses. It will also help them to form good dictionary habits early in life—to understand alphabetical order, to develop speed in finding words, appreciation for the meanings of words and sensitivity for their correct usage.

The *Golden Dictionary* is intended to help these attitudes and habits to get started through a dictionary content that is picturesque and not too complex for children to understand. The definitions have been presented in lively form, using situations from the child's everyday world. Colour has been used on every page. Each of the more than 1,500 definitive illustrations attracts the child's interest and holds his attention.

Let the child become acquainted with his dictionary casually. Encourage him to explore it by himself and to ask questions. Guide him gradually to take his questions directly to the book and try to find the answers there. He should have plenty of time to examine the pictures, to think about the meanings of the words, and to experiment with the uses of the words. He may want to make a dictionary of his own with new words he has learned and wants to learn more about.

❋❋

THE YOUNG CHILD

Children who cannot read will enjoy the pictures in the book. The pictures will help them to learn to associate names with objects. Even three-year-olds point to objects that they recognise and shout their names. They say, "What is that?" and "What is he doing?" about pictures they do not understand at first glance. The four-year-olds may discover the alphabet and learn to recognise words beginning in "A" and words beginning with "B" and the other letters of the alphabet.

❋❋

THE OLDER CHILD

The child of kindergarten or primary-school age is likely to feel more at home with books and will probably find both pictures and words more familiar. He will be more able to use the book by himself and to ask the proper questions to find out what he doesn't know. And he will be ready to learn new ways of using this new book.

Many children of primary-school age are ready to play games with words. They may name animals and objects. They may call out words and have one of the children try to find them in the dictionary. At this stage some may need help in learning the alphabet.

A FIRST LANGUAGE BOOK

The *Golden Dictionary* is a first tool for the young child to use as he is taking his beginning steps in attaining a dictionary habit. If his interests are aroused, if he is skilfully guided, and if he gains satisfaction from his experience with this book, he will want to continue his explorations among words, and will soon be ready for a more advanced dictionary.

❋❋

THE SELECTION OF WORDS

There are only 1,030 words defined in The *Golden Dictionary*, so the entire contents is well within the grasp of a child who is given some help in exploring it. However, this basic vocabulary has been greatly enlarged and enriched by several methods. There are 888 variants of the 1,030 main words, including plurals of nouns, comparative forms of adjectives, principal parts of verbs, related forms of pronouns, and some compound words (such as *playmate* under *play*) which appear in the definitions. The most unusual feature of the book is that of the grouped words under basic concepts, such as *acts*, *animals*, *foods*, and *machines*. The 322 words which fall into these classes are all illustrated and form a valuable addition to the child's working vocabulary though they are not, in most cases, included among the alphabetical entries.

❋❋

DEFINING THE WORDS

In defining the words for The *Golden Dictionary*, a great deal of thought was exercised to use only words which were included in the vocabulary of The *Golden Dictionary*. Of course there are some exceptions, but actually very few. Only those meanings which, in the opinion of the author and editors, would be understood by a young child, have been presented. Where several different and distinct meanings of a single root word have been presented—for example, see *plant*—the different meanings are numbered, 1, 2, 3, so that the child will see them as separate ideas.

Synonyms have been avoided in general. Abstract words like *number, measure,* and *thing* have been defined with special care. As far as possible, every word is presented in an interesting and exciting situation, familiar to a child.

❋❋

THE ILLUSTRATIONS

In illustrating The *Golden Dictionary*, infinite care has been taken by the artist to create a correct as well as an appealing picture for the word. These pictures add greatly to the child's skill in discovering and understanding the meanings of the words and colour has been used to assist in the definition of many words.